GLOBALIZE TO MONETIZE

Taking Your Online Business

To New Markets

GABRIELA TAYLOR

Legal Notice

All Rights Reserved

Contents

Introduction

The most remarkable aspect of taking your business online is that it is accessible by everyone and anyone across the globe. However, just because it is possible for businesses to reach people in different countries does not mean that all the potential customers in these countries will be receptive to the message that you are relaying. As such, when you take your business global, it is important that you optimize your website to accommodate the anticipated barriers and logistics of dealing with diverse countries and international requirements. It is also important that you understand the cultural differences when it comes to marketing strategies and consumer purchasing patterns.

Throughout this book I will cover some of the most important aspects to consider when marketing your online business to new global markets. These aspects are listed below and will be covered in detail for each region: North America, Europe, Asia, Latin America, Australia & New Zealand and Middle East & North Africa.

1. Website Content And Layout

Site content is an essential factor for every online business. Creating content that is relevant and specific to your international audience requires a reliable content management system (CMS). Content management systems will aid you in generating content that will appeal to the needs and tastes of the different global site users. The best content management systems are those that can function through just one login for all the country domains that are represented on your site. And speaking of domains, consider having domain names that are country specific; as such, you will avoid the high bounce rates that are likely to occur when you have a single site that may give site visitors the impression that their language or country is not catered for in your local website. Also make sure that Google knows where you want to show your site by specifying it in Google Webmaster Tools.

Language is another important factor to take into consideration when launching a global online website. Site users are more likely to purchase your goods or services if the website accommodates their language. Also bear in mind that not all the languages read left-to-right like the Latin languages; there is Arabic and Hebrew that read right-to-left and Chinese, Japanese and Korean that read both, horizontally and vertically. If the Asian characters appear horizontally then they will be read from left-to-right, just like English. If they appear vertically, usually on banners and shop signs, then they will read from top to bottom and from right-to-left.

Admittedly, making your site language friendly by translating it into different languages can be a costly investment. To do this cost-effectively, consider translating your site partially or offering country specific pages that cater to the countries with which you make the most transactions. You may also use 'Simplified English Technology', which simplifies the English text on your site so that even Non-native English speakers are able to understand the site content.

The following is a list of the most spoken languages online according to internetworldstats.com. The highest increase in language adoption online in the last 10 years has been seen with languages such as Arabic (2,500% increase), Russian (1,800% increase) and Chinese (1,500% increase).

TOP TEN LANGUAGES IN THE INTERNET	Internet Users by Language
English	565,004,126
Chinese	509,965,013
Spanish	164,968,742
Japanese	99,182,000
Portuguese	82,586,600
German	75,422,674
Arabic	65,365,400
French	59,779,525
Russian	59,700,000
Korean	39,440,000
TOP 10 LANGUAGES	1,615,957,333
Rest of the Languages	350,557,483
WORLD TOTAL	2,099,926,965

It is essential that you consider local differences at the onset of your site design efforts. For example different languages can have different word lengths for the same word. Instead of creating one single field length for the different languages on your site that you have to keep adjusting, it is a good idea to input codes that will allow your site to accommodate different word lengths automatically. Consider this: if you have a German audience, the words they will use will be approximately 30% lengthier in comparison to similar

English words; meanwhile words in Japanese will be 30% shorter.

The same applies when creating your AdWords campaigns. Double-width characters (Chinese, Japanese, Korean, Arabic and Hebrew) need nearly twice the display space as single-byte characters (Latin languages). So while an ad with single-byte characters will have 25 characters in the title, 35 in the first and second line description and 35 in the display URL, an ad with double-width characters will only have 12 characters in the title, 17 in the first and second line description and 35 in the display URL (note that only single-width characters are allowed in the display URL).

2. Cultural Considerations

Optimizing the language aspect of your site is a good first step, but you also need to take into consideration the role of images, colors and videos. Different colors and images may mean different things to the various cultures. You do not want to repel potential clients by using colors and images that may be offensive. This requires research and an understanding of the various global symbolisms of different cultures. For video, consider including subtitles and language specific voiceovers to ensure that your international site users gain the most value from your website.

3. Internationally Friendly Shopping Cart

Because you are dealing with international clients, it is essential that you optimize the shopping cart experience. This entails taking into consideration the currency differences in each country and the appropriate conversion rates. Although it might not be practicable to accommodate all the international currencies, it is a good idea to analyze the types of clients that you transact with frequently and then offer services for payment through their currency. Also integrate API (Application Programming Interface) tools into your website to provide customers with an easily accessible method of converting currencies and determining the prevailing exchange rates. An example of a reliable API is the *Exchange Rate API*.

Some of the major world currencies that you should consider adding on the site for your customers include:

US Dollar (USD)

British Pound (GBP)

Euro (EUR)

Japanese Yen (JPY)

Australian Dollar (AUD)

Hong Kong Dollar (HKD)

Swiss Franc (CHF)

Canadian Dollar (CAD)

Swedish Krone (SEK)

South Korean Won (KRW)

Indian Rupee (INR)

Chinese Yuan (CNY)

4. Distribution And Shipping Costs

International shipping takes longer and costs more than shipping domestically. The international economy is particularly problematic because the rules of trade are very different, for example taxation rules and tariff rates. Additionally there are also differences in currencies that make global shipping and distribution even more complex. Most online global retailers use web based shipping management software that allows them to determine the landing rates and the delivery time of the products that they ship to their clients worldwide. The best providers of such software include *UPS, FedEx, E4X Inc and Kewill Systems Plc.* Landing rates are costs that include custom duties and tariff rates in the customer's country. Be sure to integrate this shipping management system into your website to ensure that international customers know the exact cost of the products that they purchase from you.

5. Export Regulations

Address the export regulations and exceptions that may apply to your country and the customers' countries. Regulations may include the need for an export license on certain products. Consider including a catalog and shopping cart restriction on the products that require export licenses or those that have import restrictions. This is applicable even if your site does not sell anything and is rather an informational site.

6. Search Engine Marketing (SEO & PPC)

As an online global business, you need to take into consideration how the targeted international market will find you through the search engines. Keyword optimization is the first thing that businesses consider when they attempt to optimize their sites for the search engines. However, you must be careful when translating keywords into multiple languages as the direct or indirect translations may vary radically from the English keywords. This requires extensive research on your part, so that you have a comprehensive list of possible keywords ('exact' and 'related') that searchers are more likely to use to query the search engines.

As you think about the search engines and try to optimize your site for international clients, take into consideration that you will be dealing with search engines other than the familiar 'Google'. Some international search engines that people from all over the world are using include Naver in South Korea, Baidu in China, Seznam in the Czech Republic, and Yandex in Russia.

In addition to optimizing your keywords, you should also consider optimizing your ads in such way that they are geo-specific. Your target audience is more likely to click through an ad that literally speaks to them through their respective language. By clicking through these ads, they will land on your site, which by now is already built to accommodate and cater to as many languages as possible.

7. International Branding And Global Campaigns

Global branding and marketing campaigning entails reaching out to the local people in the countries that your business serves. It entails localizing your product offering and your brand in such a way that the local people can relate to it. Global campaigns make brands that were known by just a handful of people become internationally recognized.

Brands such as Nike are known in virtually every country; this is because the sports gear and personal apparel that are the main products from Nike are tailored to have both, a local and international appeal. Nike's global ad campaigns are hardly ever the same from country to country. Instead, the ads tend to mesh well with the local trends, needs and tastes of the countries that Nike serves.

As you launch your global business, there are various factors that you must take into consideration to establish a brand name that resonates well with audiences across the global marketplace.

Consider your market: As you venture out to cater to an international audience, your global ads and marketing campaigns must consider local market dynamics. Do you have a strong market that needs the products you are offering? Who are your competitors and are they too tough to compete with? How loyal are the locals to your competitors and do you have a strategy of winning the local market over from your competitors? For your global campaign to be successful, the local people must see value in what you are offering them.

Naming your products and services: In selecting a name for your services or products, it is important that you are sensitive to the local culture. When selling to international markets, use product names that relate and resonate well with the locals, names that make sense to them and names that they are attached to. To do this you might require a local person to help you in determining the most suitable product names to use. However, you can also retain the English name of your product to cater to the English speaking audiences.

Logos and Images: As you advertise and market your business in international markets, your logo will be primarily visible to your target market. After all, this is how your target market will associate with your brand. Thus, it is important that you adapt your logo and any images that accompany your ads and marketing campaigns to suit the local expectations. This will ensure that you do not put up a global campaign that is tainted with offensive images that may convey a different message from what you are really looking to communicate.

The message: A global campaign for your business is all about crafting and conveying the right message. This will come across through the creativity behind ads and the strategies behind your sales and marketing. You might have to engage the services of a local advertising and public relations firm to create the right message for the local audience and the appropriate channels for delivering this message. Again, ensure that you take into consideration the cultural differences in the different countries that you are catering

11

for. It does not pay to launch an aggressive global campaign that is virtually the same in every country and if you do not understand the cultural differences of your target markets, your marketing campaigns can end up having a detrimental effect.

1

Short Introduction To Online Marketing

Online Marketing is also known as 'Internet Marketing' or 'Digital Marketing'. Internet Marketing entails marketing product and service offerings as well as increasing brand awareness through the Internet. While one may think that all it takes to launch a successful Internet marketing campaign is setting up a website, this is just one aspect of it.

Internet Marketing is a relatively new concept in business marketing that has only caught up given the tremendous growth in web users worldwide; more than 30% of the world's population is now online. Internet Marketing has allowed brands to transcend boundaries at limited costs when compared to traditional forms of marketing. While online marketing presents greater opportunities to reach a worldwide audience, the competition is indeed fierce. Marketers thus adopt various forms of online marketing to ensure that they are really engaging with their target audience and overcoming the competition.

The Main Online Marketing Techniques

are: SEO, PPC, Social Media, Affiliate Marketing, Display Advertising, Video and Mobile.

Search Engine Marketing (SEM): This involves both search engine optimization (SEO) and pay-per-click (PPC) techniques.

SEO are marketing techniques that help to enhance a website's visibility at the search engine page results. This technique of Internet marketing takes into consideration the search phrases that searchers use when looking for something online. To optimize a site, a marketer would need to create content that is relevant to the keywords that searchers are likely to use to query the search engines. Additionally, including backlinks from authoritative sites is important for boosting a website's rankings at the search engines, and in effect makes the website more visible to the target audience.

Pay-Per-Click Advertising is a form of contextual marketing and paid inclusion. This method of online marketing entails promoting a site by bidding for keywords and paying for the best keywords that are likely to rank a page highly at the search engines.

Article Marketing And Directory Listing: Article marketing is part of SEO and entails the creation of niche specific articles and then posting them on either your blog or other web article directories. This can be an effective method of attracting traffic back to a site and for creating valuable backlinks. The main aim of article marketing is not to sell directly to people but to offer them relevant information that indicates your expertise and in effect prompt your audience to visit your website.

Social Media Marketing: This type of Internet marketing has only recently become popular due to the sheer number of web users engaged in social networks. This type of marketing online entails using social media platforms such as Facebook, Twitter, Pinterest, Google+ and YouTube among others to market a product, service or brand. Social media marketing is proving to be a viable method of reaching out to targeted audiences and engaging with them on a more personal level.

Affiliate Marketing: This method of online marketing entails the creation of an affiliate program in which a business awards individuals who collaborate with the business to promote the site or products. When an affiliate brings a visitor to the business site, the affiliate is rewarded.

As an Internet marketing technique, affiliate marketing has the potential to increase site traffic as well as sales, when done strategically.

Video marketing: This entails the creation and distribution of promotional videos to a targeted audience. Online video marketing can be an effective channel of increasing brand awareness and attracting significant amount of traffic to a business. Online videos are more appealing and visually engaging for a large majority of online consumers compared to textual promotional messages. Online videos are also very shareable, allowing marketers to enjoy a wide reach with their video content.

Email marketing: This is the use of electronic mail to directly market to a target audience. This form of marketing entails building a list of potential customers and leads, and then sending targeted messages to those on the list. Specifically, email marketing entails sending out promotional emails to potential clients with the aim of converting them into buying customers. Marketers also use email marketing to boost customer loyalty and for relationship building with customers. Email marketing may also entail placing your advertisement in emails sent out by other marketers in a complementing niche.

Advantages Of Internet Marketing

No Geographical Boundaries: The Internet offers a great platform for marketers looking to reach a wide audience. Because the Internet doesn't have geographical boundaries, consumers from all over the world can access your products and services without the need to interact physically. Thus, in addition to marketing and doing business locally, many businesses even small ones, can easily reach the overseas markets.

Cost Savings: Internet marketing has made doing business more cost effective. Unlike traditional marketing that requires large budgets yet reaches only a few people, Internet marketing reaches a larger audience at a lower cost.

Ongoing Business: Internet marketing means that you can reach your target audience twenty-four hours, seven days a week. Customers can access your company websites, view and purchase products anytime regardless of the time differences. This ongoing access places online business at a greater advantage compared to a solely brick-and-mortar business.

Display Of Detailed Information: Unlike traditional marketing, Internet Marketing enables marketers to offer all the information their target audience may require to make a purchasing decision. Websites offer a dynamic platform for businesses to build trust with customers who can easily access information and make inquiries about products and services that interest them.

Tapping Into New Markets: Sometimes marketers can leave out a certain market segment, because they are simply unaware of this segment. However, Internet Marketing makes it possible for this untapped market to find the business and the products it is offering, by simply searching online.

Access To More Tools: Internet Marketing is very dynamic. Marketers have access to a myriad of tools to market a website along with the product offering. These tools, such as mobile applications and social media, make it possible for marketers to reach out to their audience, engage with them, find out what their interests are and tailor their products to the needs of their customers. It is also much easier and cheaper now for Internet marketers to conduct research, analyze their markets and monitor their progress.

Worldwide User Demographics

According to Internet World Stats, there were 2.3 billion web users worldwide by the first quarter of 2012. China in Asia hosts the largest number of Internet users with more than 513 million users.

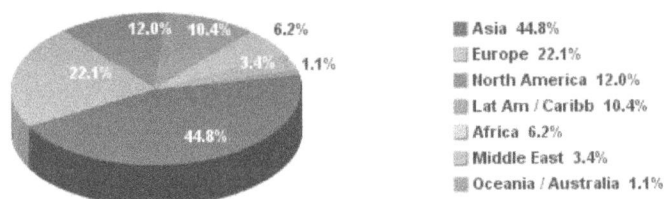

Internet Users in the World
Distribution by World Regions - 2011

- Asia 44.8%
- Europe 22.1%
- North America 12.0%
- Lat Am / Caribb 10.4%
- Africa 6.2%
- Middle East 3.4%
- Oceania / Australia 1.1%

Source: Internet World Stats - www.internetworldstats.com/stats.htm
Basis: 2,267,233,742 Internet users on December 31, 2011
Copyright © 2012, Miniwatts Marketing Group

Internet World Stats also shows that Iceland in Europe has the highest Internet penetration with up to 98% of it population using the Internet.

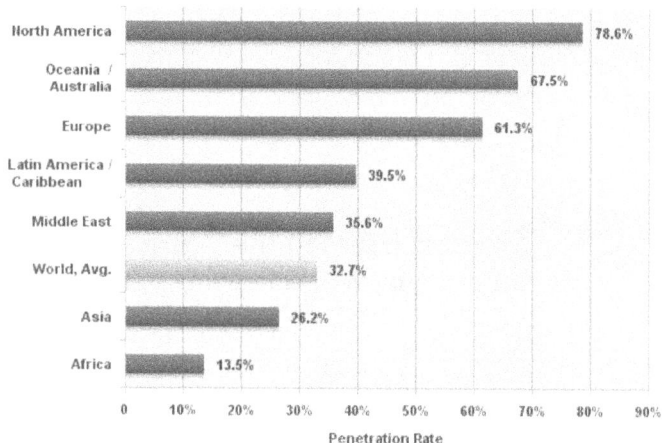

**World Internet Penetration Rates
by Geographic Regions - 2011**

Source: Internet World Stats - www.internetworldststs.com/stats.htm
Penetration Rates are based on a world population of 6,930,055,154
and 2,267,233,742 estimated Internet users on December 31, 2011.
Copyright © 2012, Miniwatts Marketing Group

Globally, Internet penetration rates have increased by up to 445% since the start of the millennium. This has allowed many businesses to reach a global audience.

Google remains the most dominant search engine globally even though some local search engines in Asia, Russia and Latin America continue to gain traction.

2

Online And Offline Marketing

Online marketing has simplified how businesses market their brands. This is especially true with regard to budgets and audience reach. More and more marketers are leveraging the benefits that come with reaching a wider audience, within a shorter period of time and at a lower cost. However, offline marketing still has its own place in business. It is more beneficial for marketers to integrate both forms of marketing instead of using just one and overlooking the other.

Offline marketing has until recently been the primary channel through which brands promoted their products or services. This includes the use of magazines and newspapers, radio and television as well as billboards. These mediums of marketing have been successful and they continue to play an important role for brand marketing and advertising. When strategically planned, offline marketing provides a venue to bring a human face to your campaign, thereby having greater interaction with your customers.

However, offline marketing can prove to be costly and difficult to measure the campaign's return on investment. Another downside to this type of marketing is that it can only reach a few people at any given time, as it is largely restricted by geographical boundaries. Additionally, offline marketers often find themselves tabulating marketing results in very broad terms. It is not always feasible to have cost effective, precise data on the effect of the offline marketing campaign.

On the other hand, online marketing offers some promising advantages. As mentioned in the previous chapter, online marketing is not limited to geographical boundaries. This allows marketers to reach as wide an audience as their marketing and business goals will allow. Reaching a wider audience through online methods is not as costly as it is with offline marketing campaigns.

Online marketing makes it feasible to track your marketing campaign with easily accessible tools. You can track the effectiveness of your campaign and key benchmarks with tools such as *Omniture, Google Analytics* and *Coremetrics*. You can also change your campaign as soon as you find out that it is not performing optimally. Due to the nature of offline campaigns, it can take a long time before assessing the real progress of your campaign. This could sometimes mean putting resources to a campaign that is unsuccessful and not finding out until it is too late.

Online marketing allows you to precisely target your audience. Offline marketing campaigns do have target audiences yet; it is likely that a large majority of this audience is not keen about the product or service being promoted. Online marketing gives you more latitude in terms of targeting a very specific group of people and marketing to them based on their demonstrated interests.

Online marketing is much more dynamic than offline marketing. Online marketing offers marketers access to a wide range of tools for marketing including search engine optimization, search marketing, social media marketing, video marketing, article marketing, blogs, ad banners and paid inclusions among others. Additionally, these tools can be tailored to your budget and target audience.

Marketing online can increase the conversion rates. It is easier to communicate and connect with targeted customers though social networks and your website than it is through a print magazine ad. This potential for connection offered by the Internet resources makes it much easier to convert your audience to buying customers.

How To Get Your Online And Offline Marketing Working Together

Using Hashtags (#): Hashtags can prove effective in analyzing the progress of your offline campaigns. Simply create a Twitter hashtag related to your offline marketing efforts. This will enable you to track the number of people who are talking about your brand and your efforts. While you cannot track offline word of mouth, you can track the online mentions you receive. There are numerous tools to use to track your hashtag mentions but one great and free tool is Hashtracking.com. This service updates hashtag mentions within twenty-four hours.

Adding URL Tracking: Admittedly, it can be difficult to monitor the effectiveness of each of your offline marketing efforts. However, integrating these efforts with the power of the web can enable you to track your offline campaign. As you use offline techniques such as print and outdoor marketing and advertising, assign a unique URL to each advertisement. These URLs redirect your audience to your website where Google Analytics will track the sources of the incoming traffic. This approach enables you to determine which segments of the incoming web page traffic are from your offline efforts.

Using Social Media For Offline Traffic: Social media has become an indispensable tool for marketers who are organizing offline events. Instead of spending too much on offline advertising and marketing of an event, publicize the event on social media networks such as Twitter and Facebook as well as your blog. Use your online social networks to tell people why they should attend the event.

Making Use Of QR Codes: QR codes are digital barcodes that allow an offline user to utilize their mobile phone to scan a code that triggers a certain action. Offline users can use QR codes to access a website, to view a video, to purchase an item or to redeem a coupon. QR codes can be a profitable tool to integrate your online and offline campaigns.

Including URLs In Offline Material: One way to get offline users to engage with your brand online is to offer them information about your online presence. Include your website URL as well as social media links in offline promotional materials such as brochures. Instead of simply adding a Twitter or Facebook logo, make your own brand more visible by displaying a link to your Twitter account or Facebook page.

Social media has transformed how offline marketers and sales teams use leads. Instead of cold calling without any information about the lead, you can use social media profiles to find out the basics about the person you are calling. Platforms such as LinkedIn can prove helpful in learning about a lead's interests and background, to allow you to build greater rapport with your prospects.

3
Types Of Online Businesses

The Internet provides a myriad of business opportunities for marketers looking to improve sales and maximize their return on investment (ROI). The online business model one chooses depends on the business goals, the funds available, the type of skills they have to implement the model as well as the relevancy and prevalence of the chosen model. While there are numerous online business models, here are some of the most common ones:

Freemium

Many online businesses look to adopt the freemium model with the assumption that in the end, they will be able to make actual sales. While the freemium model can be effective in garnering a user base, it needs a strategic approach. Contrary to popular belief, this type of model does not entail giving out products or services free. It means that most of your audience uses the product free while the minority pays for it.

To get the freemium model working for you, you need to attract plenty of users. At the heart of this model is sheer numbers, so that you are able to increase the minority percentage that will pay for a product or service.

Once you get the users, you need to find ways of keeping them around. This requires that you find out the things that interest the users and will make them continue to engage with you. You also need to have a product or service that increases in value from the users' point of view. This ensures that over time, more and more users will be inclined to pay for a product that they feel is valuable to them.

To benefit from the freemium model, it is particularly important that you keep the costs of operation low. Because you are offering the basic product or services free, your profit margins are likely to be narrow. Thus, keeping your costs low ensures that your business is still able to run on the low profit margins.

Admittedly, it will take a long time before your business is profitable if you are going to use the freemium model. Nevertheless, once you build brand loyalty, it becomes easier to convert users into actual buyers. A viable approach would be to seek equity finance that can keep the business afloat until it attains the break-even point.

Examples of online business that have succeeded with the freemium model include Skype, Evernote, LinkedIn, Flickr, and Dropbox.

Advertising

Earning money through Internet advertisements is one of the oldest and most popular methods of earning money online. Once you set up your website and you have been able to attract significant traffic, the next step is to monetize and one way to do this is through advertisements.

You can do this through cost per impressions (CPM model), in which advertising networks pay you for the number of impressions your website generates for the ads placed on it. Success in earning money this way requires that you generate high quality content that attracts a large number of web users to your site. For example, if your website attracts 100,000 monthly page views and displays an ad banner that costs $2.5, your revenue per month totals to $250. Numerous advertising networks pay highly based on click per impression. However, most will pay an average of $1 and $3. The rates will also vary with the format and position of the ad. This model is suitable for bloggers who attract more than 1,000 site visitors.

Some great platforms for monetizing your online presence include:

AdPepper Media: This is one of the most popular, independent online advertising networks. The company offers online ad displays, affiliate and email marketing services and all that entails online advertising.

Tribal Fusion: This advertising network offers some of the highest click per impression rates. They specifically work with established advertisers, thus guaranteeing its online publishers immediate and attractive payments. The company pays publishers up to 55% of the advertisement revenue that your site generates.

Banner Connect: This advertisement network is widely used by Internet marketers. They have more than 7,000 publishers worldwide and they match up publishers with suitable advertisers to feature on their websites.

Google AdSense: This is also a popular method for web publishers to display complimenting textual ads on their websites and subsequently to earn profits. The ads displayed on your website are usually relevant to the type of visitors who come to your site. The amount that you earn through the Google AdSense program largely depends on the amount that advertisers pay. The amount you receive is also dependent on the keyword usage. If advertisers who displays on your site choose and pay for high paying keywords, then it is possible to receive more from advertisements. Google AdSense works based on cost-per-click so that publishers are paid when site visitors click through the advertisements displayed on the site.

Recurring Subscriptions

Paywall is a structure that keeps web users from accessing content on web pages, unless they pay a subscription fee. There are soft paywalls that allow users to view some content without paying for subscription and then gain access to the premium product, the personalized service or the complete publication after subscribing. Hard paywalls allow very minimal or no access to a product/service without subscribing.

While this method was initially popular with magazines and newspapers, many businesses with an online presence are now leveraging this model. Instead of selling products/services one at a time or individually, recurring subscriptions involve selling products/services on a monthly, annual or seasonal basis. These fees are deducted automatically from a user's appointed payment method until the users withdraws from the subscription.

Users can pay a one-time subscription fee to access a product over a given period, for example a monthly newsletter or a comprehensive report. If you are in the services business industry, you can now offer online services such as consulting, coaching, freelancing, training and speaking. Marketers may also offer unlimited subscription in which users pay a fee to access unlimited products/services or where they can transfer their user rights to family or any designated group.

This online business model can be beneficial to businesses because they can enjoy the predictability in terms of revenues as long as users stay subscribed. It can also be an effective way to build brand loyalty among consumers who can then continue to pay for the service/product. Businesses that successfully implement the recurring subscription model typically have funds available at any given time, as long as users are still subscribed. For consumers this model might offer convenience especially if they have subscribed to a service or product they regularly need.

While recurring subscriptions can offer certain benefits to businesses, online marketers need to offer value to attract their audience to subscribe and to keep their subscription going.

Micropayments

Like recurring subscriptions, micropayment works through charging users a small amount to gain access to certain web content on a one-time basis. This is certainly an alternative to offering content free or asking web users to subscribe.

Micropayments give web users the freedom of not being affiliated with a certain publication while at the same time allows the publisher to remain in business. The concept behind micropayment is that the small amounts charged on each consumer will go a long way in keeping the publication alive. It is important that businesses looking to use this model offer an easy to use payment infrastructure to avoid putting customers off. The more complex the payment method is, the likelier that potential users will turn away to another source.

Commission Payments

The most common method of commission payments model is affiliate marketing. This method involves a company creating products/services, and then an affiliate marketer collaborates with the company to promote these products/services. When someone purchases the products, the affiliate marketer receives a commission for the role they have played in prompting the sale. As a business, creating an affiliate program presents a viable method of potentially increasing sales. For an affiliate marketer, this can be a potentially lucrative channel for earning money online.

Ecommerce Stores

Another type of online business is an ecommerce store where you can sell your own products (digital or physical) or someone else's products through drop-shipping. When selling your own products you need to make sure that you have enough space to house the products and once an order is placed, you need to ship them to your customers. With the drop-shipping model, the manufacturer will house the products and also ship them; you will only need to provide the online platform where customers can choose the products they would like to purchase and where they can pay. Once an order is placed, you need to pay the manufacturer the agreed amount for the product and shipping and he will take care of the rest. Ultimately you act as a middleman who attracts the customers, sells the products but have none of the hassle of housing or shipping the goods.

You can also set up your own store on eBay or Amazon and sell products provided by worldwide suppliers found on Alibaba.com and WorldwideBrands.com

The App Model

The App model for online business entails the creation of applications for use by smartphone users as well as for desktop use. After developing an application, you can either distribute it as a free or paid application. It is possible to make money through both free and paid applications.

In the case of paid applications for mobile phones, for example, the applications are paid for in incremental terms. These prices start from as low as $0.99 and increase incrementally. When using Apple as your app store front, you can receive as much as 30% of each app you sell. While the individual app sales may seem negligible, the cumulative sales can net you significant revenue.

The greatest advantage of selling your application is the potential to generate income. Additionally app stores such as Apple are more receptive to paid applications than they are to free ones.

The major source of income for free applications is pay-per-click advertising, which works on a similar premise as AdSense. It is also possible to make money with in-app spends or by using the free application as a preview for the paid variation of the application. You can use various advertising companies to add advertisements into your free application. These include *Google Adsense, GreyStripe, iAd, Admob, Brightroll*, among others.

The most attractive benefit of free apps is that you can continue to make money even after people have downloaded the application. On the contrary, paid apps only allow you to make money once, when the application is bought, unless it features in-app advertisements. You are also more likely to reach a greater audience because more people are inclined to download a free application than they are with a paid one.

APIs And Access to Data

An Application Programming Interface is a source code interface created and offered for other users to use it. An example of an API is Google Maps, which hosts snippets of data that relate to geo-location and mapping. Another great example is Facebook applications.

Through an API, developers can create applications that enhance users' experience. Through APIs, websites are able to communicate with each other and use each other's technological creations to come up with inventive products. One of the benefits of creating an open or free API is that it has the capacity to create backlinks to your website. This can go a long way in boosting your rankings at the search engines, thereby generating free marketing for your website and your business.

It is important that you limit the number of APIs you create and distribute, especially if you are looking to make money through the APIs. Limiting your APIs creates a demand for them, allowing you to charge a premium price to users who are interested in the API.

This model of online business offers companies the opportunity to specialize at a single stage of the data-access value chain. This is because the production or creation of data is typically a complex and intensive process that entails the use of human and technological resources. Nevertheless, once this data is developed, you are able to sell it to other users who will then develop the application further and perhaps sell it to other users down the value chain.

Application Programming Interfaces offer companies the opportunity to utilize web resources to release their processed output in a way that they themselves can control. In this way you, as the data publisher are in a position to provide the data freely for all users to access without jeopardizing your profit margins.

I've summarized the most common types of businesses you can find online. In the next chapters we will see how online marketing differs from one country to another and what you need to do in order to succeed in a global online environment.

4

Online Marketing In North America

North America (US and Canada) is rightfully seen as the center of global business and is the third biggest Internet market after Asia and Europe with 275 million users according to internetworldstats.com.

The developed online infrastructure (with 78% Internet penetration and ranked 12th in terms of Internet connection speed) may present a great opportunity for expanding your business to North America. However, this will not be without the typical challenges facing global business today. Here is how to navigate the North American market:

Cultural Differences: Do's And Dont's

The North American societies of Canada and USA provides 13% of the worldwide Internet users and are made up of a wide variety of ethnic groups and cultures. Each of these groups are likely to have a different reception and perception of your marketing messages. While it is laudable to simply cater to the mainstream North American market, it is also important to take into consideration the needs and inflections of other cultural groups in the country. Thus, it is a good idea to determine which markets you really want to target and then create marketing messages that are ethnically and culturally appropriate to this group. English is the main language in the region and also the most spoken language online, however 1 in 5 Americans speak a foreign language at home other than English.

If you need to reach out to the Latino market in the U.S. for example, you might have to use Spanish in constructing your marketing message. While many Latinos feel that they are part of mainstream America, they might find it offensive if the marketing message used to reach them does not portray a true picture of them. The proportion of the U.S. population that currently speaks Spanish as a first language sits at 16% (see table of the top 10 countries by number of Spanish speakers). By 2050 it is expected that Hispanics will constitute 30%+ of the U.S. population. As you can see in the following table there are now more Spanish speakers in the U.S. than in Spain.

Country	Country Population	Spanish Native Speakers	Spanish Second Language	Percentage Population	Total Spanish Speakers
Mexico	112,396,211	103,527,885	7,110,031	98.5%	110,637,916
U.S.A.	309,059,724	44,468,501	6,231,499	15.8%	50,700,000
Spain	47,021,031	41,848,717	4,581,088	98.8%	46,456,779
Colombia	45,783,000	45,338,905	77,831	99.2%	45,416,736
Argentina	40,900,496	39,608,040	1,047,053	99.4%	40,655,093
Venezuela	29,056,000	28,033,228	674,100	98.8%	28,707,328
Peru	29,797,694	23,769,620	2,035,183	86.6%	25,804,803
Chile	17,248,450	15,513,255	1,600,024	99.3%	17,127,711
Ecuador	14,306,000	13,298,858	733,324	98.1%	14,024,376
Guatemala	14,361,666	9,291,997	3,116,482	86.4%	12,408,479

In Canada, French is the mother tongue of about 23% of the population, while English is the mother tongue of 60% of the population. The French speakers in Quebec are more independent and want to be approached as an independent group/province, rather than as a collectivity of the entire country. According to comScore, Canada is the most engaged nation globally (ahead of the U.S. and the UK) with the most time spent online (45+ hours per visitor monthly) and with the highest number of pages visited per visitor (4,000+ pages per visitor monthly).

As you seek to do business in North America, consider that Americans have a very direct way of communicating. They appreciate processes that are logical and linear and thus they expect that others will be direct and clear in their communication as well. As you present your marketing message, make it very clear, logical and easy for your audience to understand. However, while Canadians think analytically and linearly, they tend to be polite and diplomatic in their communicational approach.

Unlike practices in Latin America, Middle East and Asia where small talk precedes business, North Americans want to get straight to the point. If you are making a presentation to your potential global partners, use data and practically demonstrate the benefit of your product. In other words, get to the point quickly while you have your audience's attention.

Virtual methods of communication are popular in this region (see the following table from exacttarget.com). This is underscored by the fact that the North Americans are typically looking for convenience and something that will save time. Thus, emails Facebook, SMS and Skype are common methods of business communication. The communication style is also less formal; if you are from a culture that values formality and subtly, it is important that you accommodate the communication style of your North American audience or business partners.

AT LEAST DAILY	AT LEAST WEEKLY	LESS THAN WEEKLY	NEVER

Email
3%
91% 5%

Facebook
1%
57% 13% 11% 19%

Text Messages
57% 11% 10% 22%

"Check In" using location-based social networking
28% 9% 11% 52%

Instant Messanger
24% 8% 16% 52%

Messaging using an app on a mobile device
19% 5% 6% 70%

Twitter
14% 6% 9% 71%

LinkedIn
10% 8% 14% 68%

If you are meeting directly with your global partners, be sure to keep time, because punctuality is particularly valued in this region. Your online global customers will also expect you to keep time in terms of delivery, solving a problem, answering inquiries. Given the importance of punctuality, many people are likely to be turned off when things are not done on time.

Unlike business in the Middle East, where contracts are not as important as the spoken word, in the U.S. and Canada a contract is the final agreement. People are more likely to take your engagement with them seriously if you have a contract with them. This applies to both your clients and local business partners. Contracts typically stipulate each party's obligations and it is expected that you keep to your end of the deal. Take into consideration that the U.S. has the highest rate of litigations and people tend to sue for just about anything.

North Americans tend to be closed in, in terms of culture and their knowledge of the outside world. Thus, universal rules are much preferred and they place a great deal of importance on experts who are typically consulted before a decision is made.

In contrast to Latin America where people are generally risk averse, North Americans are open to change, new ideas, new products and new ways of doing as long as these offer convenience.

Gift giving is not considered appropriate in the region and this may be seen as bribing your audience or business partners.

Website Design And Customer Engagement

As you create a website for the North American audience, take into consideration the mainstream culture and the elements that are likely to appeal to this audience. It is also important that you consider your target audience in terms of their age, their interests, income status, and demographics.

Typically the younger audience in the region will be more attracted by animations and graphics splashed all over the pages. This market segment is looking for an easy to use interface but at the same time a site that calls for greater engagement. While, a clean site might appeal to an older or corporate audience, it might not cut it for the younger generation.

The corporate market is another segment that you need to have in mind when designing your website. A website targeting this market segment calls for a less cluttered interface, web pages that offer adequate information about a brand and its products and how your audience can go about getting or using the product. While an Asian website will feature multiple links, a website for Americans typically features fewer links that take the site users directly to the information they are looking for. Intense graphics and animation are less appealing for the corporate market segment. A representation of your brand or products is more appreciated instead.

If you are going to include music on the website, choose music that is appropriately suited to your target audience. While Europeans may be irritated by background music on a website, Americans are more easy-going and will generally accept music as long as it is inoffensive and relevant. Canadians are more likely to appreciate less raucous music.

The North American audience tends to be avid searchers of information. Features such as testimonials are very important to this audience even though the society is inclined to individual decision-making. Testimonials are very common on American and Canadian websites as a way of establishing trust and of proving the authenticity of a brand and its products. According to demandforce.com 70% of consumers trust a brand with a minimum of 6 to 10 reviews and 50% of the U.S. shoppers will not buy if a product got less than 3 stars rating.

The audience in this region is generally more willing to share their information, than the audience in Western Europe is. However, North Americans are strict with their privacy and they expect people to keep boundaries and respect their privacy. While they offer their information easily, they also withdraw this information easily if they perceive that their privacy is infringed upon. Canadians are more willing to give out information once they have established a sense of trust with a person.

Colors and their symbolism will play a great role in your website design considerations for the North American audience.

Bright **red** is likely to catch your audience's attention fast. Red represents passion. It can be used to stimulate attention and appetite, but when overused it can convey a message of danger or urgency. It is important that you use the red color moderately.

Orange brings a sense of energy, celebration and festivity. It also symbolizes bounty and harvest and it can be used appropriately for just about any target market, but more specifically for the younger audience. You might have noticed that most apps created to improve productivity utilize color orange to symbolize energy.

Yellow, like orange, is a color of happiness and can be used in web designs that are looking to bring out an energetic and optimistic feel.

Green is associated with nature, organic, relaxation and is appropriate for websites inspired by nature and related elements.

Blue, like green is a safe color to use especially for the older or corporate audience.

Pink is also a common color in North American websites and is primarily alluring to the female audience.

Search Engine Marketing (SEO & PPC)

An important consideration for search engine optimization (SEO) campaigns for the North American audience is localizing for each state or province that you target in your online marketing campaign. This is especially important if you are looking to target an audience in a specific state/province. One basic way to do this is to include the name of the state/province in your web content to allow your site to appear in the local searches. For example if you were targeting an audience in New York, you would include New York or NY in your web copy. The same goes if you were localizing for Vancouver in Canada, you would naturally include the abbreviations VA and the term Vancouver in your web copy.

Top-level domains are also a crucial factor for SEO in North America. You can even use state or province specific domain names such as .nyc for New York City or .la for Los Angeles. To use the top-level domains in each country, your business may need to have a bona fide presence in the country. In Canada, you can register a domain name for a minimum period of 1 year and a maximum period of 10 year. You will also need to comply with the Canadian Presence Requirements for domain registrants.

Given that North America is made up of different ethnic groups, you might consider localizing your website for these groups if they are your primary target audience. For example, in the U.S., the Hispanics are the second largest consumer segment in the country after the non-Hispanic white segment. This means that the Hispanic market segment is one that marketers looking to reach out to the U.S. market cannot ignore. While the large majority of Hispanics in the U.S. speak English (more than 50%), an appropriate SEO campaign should seek to localize the website for the Spanish language. A good approach is to create a website that offers both Spanish and English based content. Even though there is no universal version of Spanish, it is possible to translate the Spanish language into a natural one that will cater to both the Hispanic and the non-Hispanic, but Spanish speaking populations in North America. It is noteworthy that the American Hispanics use longer words in their search phrases and queries than other web users in the country. For Canada, you would also need to include French, as the language is equally significant in the country (23% of the population).

According to a study by Econsultancy and Search Engine Marketing Professional organization, Search Engine Marketing spending continues to grow in North America, having increased by 2.7 billion in 2011. Search engine marketing budgets have particularly increased for paid search, search engine optimization, Facebook pay-per-click advertising, search technology and mobile Internet.

Mobile Internet has had the most significant impact on search marketing trends in the region. This can be attributed to the high rates of mobile and mobile Internet penetration in North America, more than any other region globally. More web users are frequently utilizing their mobile phones to access the Internet. Marketers have taken notice of this trend and are increasingly optimizing their websites for mobile to allow their target audience to easily search and find these websites on their mobile devices. According to the survey, up to 79% of companies, acknowledge the impact that mobile is having on search marketing trends in the region and are looking to leverage these trends.

In North America, SEO outsourcing is increasingly popular as more and more SEO agencies invest in outsourced services than on their in-house SEO operations. However, businesses are still spending a significant amount of their marketing budgets on SEO with up to 55% of businesses planning to increase spending for their SEO campaigns. Organic search optimization tends to be more popular than paid-per-click and social media marketing campaigns in the region.

The merging of Microsoft and Yahoo search engines has played an important role for search in the region. Up to 27% of marketers in the study say that this merging has boosted return on investment, underscored by more competitive bid prices and exposure to a wider user base. In both Canada and US, marketers largely use Google's local-based ads as well as ad sitelinks.

The role of social media in search marketing trends in the region cannot be overlooked. Marketers understand the widespread usage and penetration rates in North America and they are increasingly integrating search-marketing campaigns with social media. The Facebook pay-per-click program is increasingly becoming a preferred advertising program among marketers in the region, and has grown by 47% in the past year alone compared to a 45% growth worldwide.

Optimizing for local search is important for marketers in this region given the diverse needs of the different audiences in both countries. Up to 34% of marketers spend their search budgets on local pay-per-click, targeting regional markets as well as cities and the sub markets in these cities. According to a press release from BIA Kelsey, the U.S. local mobile search will surpass the desktop local search by 2015.

In North America, Google is the most dominant platform for pay-per-click campaigns with more than 95% of marketers using Google AdWords. According to Marin Software, in the U.S. smartphones lead tablets and computers in high click through rate and low cost per click.

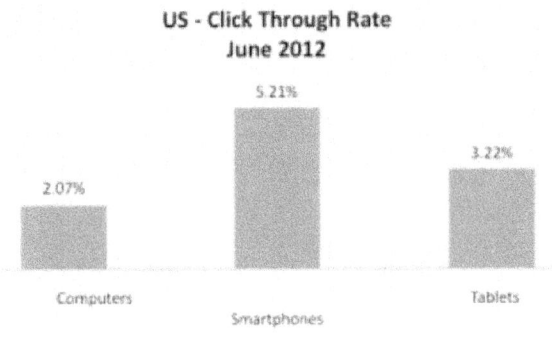

US - Click Through Rate
June 2012

5.21%

3.22%

2.07%

Computers

Smartphones

Tablets

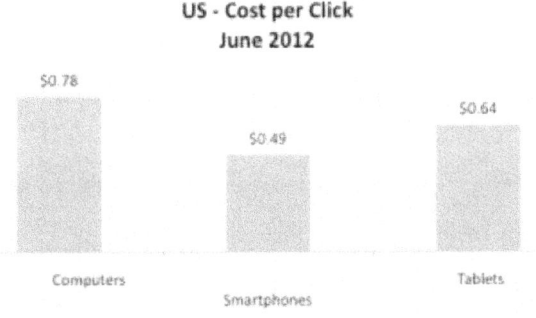

US - Cost per Click
June 2012

$0.78

$0.64

$0.49

Computers

Smartphones

Tablets

Google is also the most popular search engine in the region even though Bing is viewed as yielding better search results compared to Google search. Up to 66% of all searches undertaken in the region are done through Google, while Bing searches account for less than 25% of all searches conducted in the region.

In the past year, the top ten searches conducted through Google, Yahoo and Bing accounted for 250 million searches.

Overall, search engines play a significant role in Internet users' web navigation behavior. While users extensively rely on search engines to find information, they are uncomfortable with targeted or personalized search. Given the inclination to privacy, users in the region are not amenable to the idea of search engines saving their search histories.

According to a report by the U.S. Direct Marketing Association, Ipsos Reid Marketing and Canadian Marketing Association, both Canadian and American marketers are increasingly spending a large amount of their budgets on digital marketing. The trend is particularly greater in Canada. Marketers are realizing the opportunities offered by digital marketing as well as the measuring feasibility that allows them to monitor the impact of digital marketing campaigns including mobile QR codes and coupons, in- video ads and general promotional online videos.

Social Media Marketing

According to a recent survey by Pew Internet, an estimated 65% of online users in North America use social networks. Up to 61% of the under 30 population on these social networking platforms log on to their accounts at least once a day, 55% of the U.S.

Facebook users access it via a mobile phone and 26% of the Americans are familiar with the 'check-in' services.

The popularity of social networks depends on the age group. While Facebook is the most popular social media for all ages, Twitter is more popular amongst the 18-31 age group and Linkedin amongst the 23-45 age group. According to consumerreports.org about 7.5 million of Facebook U.S. users are under the age of 13.

"Which social networking sites do you have an account with?"							
	Gen Z (18-22)	Gen Y (23-31)	Gen X (32-45)	Younger Boomers (46-55)	Older Boomers (56-66)	Golden Generation (67+)	Total US online adults
Facebook	98%	97%	95%	95%	95%	98%	96%
Linkedin	15%	31%	35%	27%	25%	17%	28%
Twitter	38%	34%	25%	15%	11%	8%	24%
MySpace	32%	31%	23%	17%	12%	7%	22%
Other social networking site	9%	7%	5%	3%	3%	2%	5%

There is also a very interesting infographic from Forrester Research that shows what different age group does online. The most active users online are the Youth, between 18 to 21, that create content such as videos and blogs, comment on content, join social networks and sign up to different sites and also watch videos and gather information.

What people are doing

Who participates (U.S. online users)

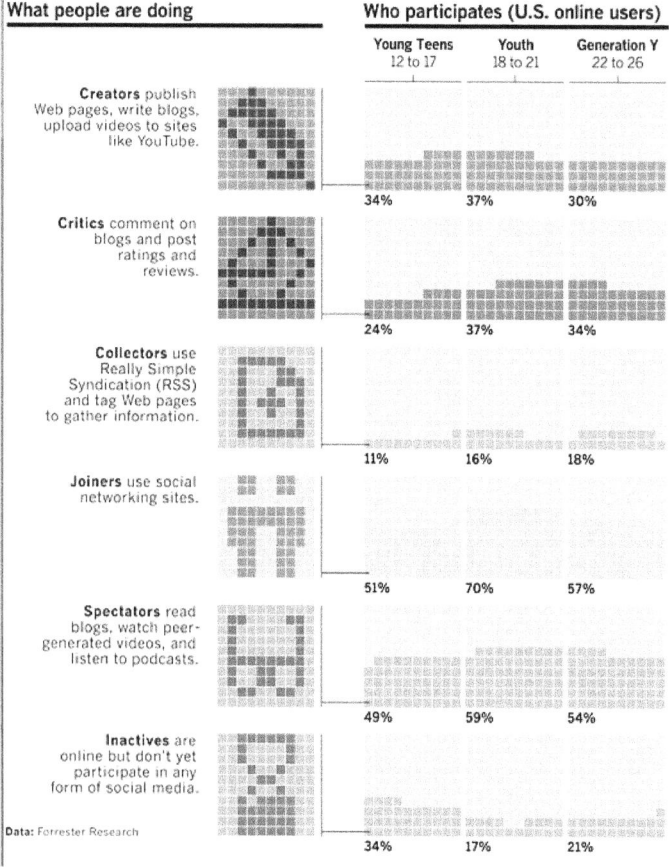

	Young Teens 12 to 17	Youth 18 to 21	Generation Y 22 to 26

Creators publish Web pages, write blogs, upload videos to sites like YouTube.

34%   37%   30%

Critics comment on blogs and post ratings and reviews.

24%   37%   34%

Collectors use Really Simple Syndication (RSS) and tag Web pages to gather information.

11%   16%   18%

Joiners use social networking sites.

51%   70%   57%

Spectators read blogs, watch peer-generated videos, and listen to podcasts.

49%   59%   54%

Inactives are online but don't yet participate in any form of social media.

Data: Forrester Research

34%   17%   21%

56

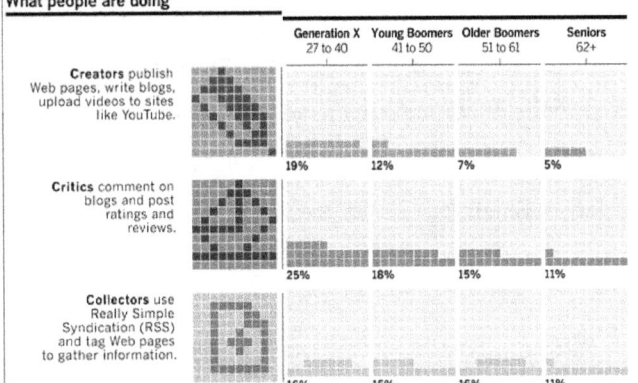

What people are doing

	Generation X 27 to 40	Young Boomers 41 to 50	Older Boomers 51 to 61	Seniors 62+
Creators publish Web pages, write blogs, upload videos to sites like YouTube.	19%	12%	7%	5%
Critics comment on blogs and post ratings and reviews.	25%	18%	15%	11%
Collectors use Really Simple Syndication (RSS) and tag Web pages to gather information.	16%	15%	16%	11%
Joiners use social networking sites.	29%	15%	8%	6%
Spectators read blogs, watch peer-generated videos, and listen to podcasts.	41%	31%	26%	19%
Inactives are online but don't yet participate in any form of social media.	42%	54%	61%	70%

Data: Forrester Research

CHART BY ARNO GHELF

North America is the top region (in terms of users) for the main social networks providing approx. 20% of the total traffic for Facebook, Twitter, Linkedin, YouTube and Google+ and more than 45% of the Pinterest's total traffic.

Businesses and online marketers are spending significant resources on social media sites, to leverage the existing audiences on these platforms. A large majority of online marketers in North America are using social media to keep track of brand mentions, to share information about a product with their audience and for indirect marketing. According to webmarketing123.com 47% of brands in the U.S. have generated leads from Facebook, 35% from Linkedin and 34% from Twitter.

HAVE YOU EVER GENERATED LEADS FROM SOCIAL MEDIA SITES (B2B and B2C)?

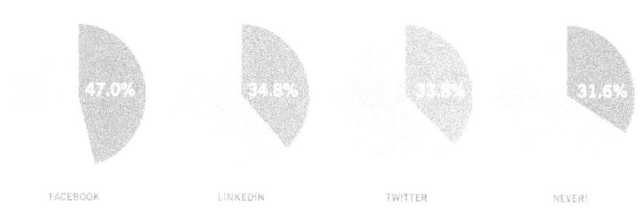

FACEBOOK   LINKEDIN   TWITTER   NEVER!

A survey by the international management-consulting firm Booz & Company and Buddy Media shows that up to 96% of businesses in the region are planning to increase their social media spend. The main priorities for leveraging social media include public relations purposes, customer service and engagement as well as marketing and promotions.

Today, 80% of the companies in the region have a presence on Facebook and an estimated 45% are using Twitter, according to a study by InSites Consulting. Overall, social media usage in North America is higher than it is in Europe. The same study shows that up to 6 out of 10 companies in the region monitor brand mentions on social medi,a while up to 80% of the companies respond to social media inquiries by their customers.

However, according to a recent survey by Edison Research an estimated 74% of users in North America do not know about mobile-based geo-location services and social networks such as FourSquare and Yelp and just about 3% of online users have used these services to 'check-in' to a business premise.

In the past two years from 2010 to present, more social network users are following brands online and specifically through social networks, with up to 33% of the online market demonstrating this trend. While the increase is laudable, the number of social media users following brands in this region is still low when compared to the users in Latin America for example.

In addition to the high social media penetration rates in North America (Facebook has a 95% penetration rate), the amount of time spent on social network sites continues to increase. Many social network users use these platforms at least once a day but often, more than once. This increasing usage offers marketers a warm audience that is available for engagement, most of the time.

Social media users in North America largely depend on social networking platforms to make purchasing decisions. In particular, users turn to Facebook for customer reviews and product recommendations before deciding to purchase something.

Email Marketing

Email marketing entails sending of promotional messages to existing customers and prospects. The primary aim of email marketing is to build relationships with clients and prospects and to create brand awareness.

In both the U.S. and Canada, there are stringent regulations pertaining to the sending of emails by marketers and soliciting of business using email marketing techniques. In the U.S., the pertinent law became applicable at the start of 2004. Unlike email regulations in the UK where marketers are prohibited to send emails to just anyone, in the U.S., marketers can send emails to anyone without their permission but the emails should include an easy way to opt-out. It is also important that emails include accurate information about the sender and the recipient; otherwise, the email will be considered 'spam'.

The Canadian anti-spam regulations require that marketers obtain explicit consent from consumers before sending them messages. The consent can be implied when there is an existing business between the marketer and the email recipient. Implied consent can last up to 2 years after the consent is actually applied.

Marketers are required to include valid information about their company and to offer a clear and simple way to unsubscribe from the email.

According to a report by Epsilon and the Direct Marketing Association, the average email marketing volumes in the region continue to show an upward growth of up to 42%. Marketers are still using email marketing to build relationships with existing clients and to engage with warm prospects.

The average open rates for emails in the region in the past year show a variation across different sectors with the open and click through rates being high for financial services marketing emails.

This is followed by the retail and travel industries, which account for a 34% and a 31% open and click rates. Email marketing messages that attract the highest click trough and open rates are those that pertain to consumer goods, retail and financial services.

A recent Forrester Research report shows that up to 89% of businesses-to-customer companies in North America are using email for marketing. A large majority of business-to-business companies also use email for marketing, accounting for an estimated 71%.

The report shows that approximately one third of email marketers remove inactive email addresses from their marketing lists. While marketers in the region continue to use email marketing, the budgets have not increased significantly compared to search engine marketing, social and mobile marketing budgets.

The Forrester report offers various recommendations for marketers looking to carry out effective marketing campaigns in the region:

a) Marketers need to invest more in tools that can help them analyze the effectiveness of their email campaigns.

Advanced analytics tools will go a long way to determining whether email messages are relevant to the recipients.

b) It is good practice for marketers to frequently clean their lists, to remain with email addresses that are likely to yield optimal results. Separating responders from the non-responders will enable marketers to focus closely on the responders or their master data list.

c) Relevance is an increasing concern among recipients of email marketing messages. Marketers need to first understand what interests their target audience before blasting out emails. Relevance is likely to improve subsequent open and click through rates.

d) Given the high mobile phone penetration rates in North America and the fact that mobile phone users are utilizing their mobile devices to access emails, it is important that marketers optimize their emails for mobile. It is necessary to make it simple for your recipients to access their email easily.

Mobile Marketing

Mobile marketing is a digital promotional method that entails sending marketing messages to targeted mobile phone users. The high mobile phone ownership rates globally have made mobile marketing a popular channel for interacting directly with customers. While SMS remains the primary mode of mobile marketing, other new forms such as GPS messaging, use of location based services and QR codes are becoming increasingly popular. More than 50% of smartphone users have watched videos on their mobile device.

Studies show that 43% of the North Americans (see graphic from Nielsen) use a smartphone and this number continues to rise. Mobile marketers are leveraging these trends to tap into the growing mobile phone user based. The mobile ads that seem to be attracting the highest click through rates are related to the travel industry and location-based advertisements powered on by tools such as Foursquare and Yelp.

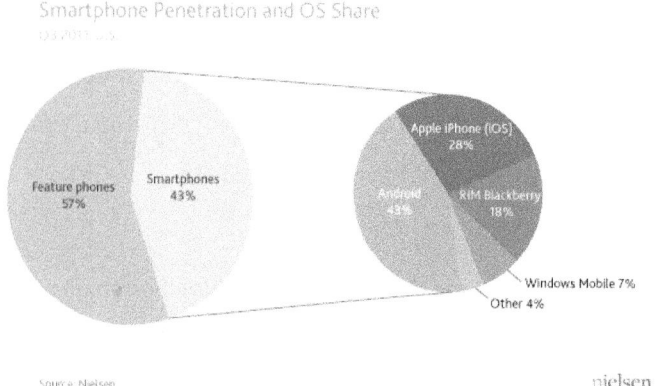

Smartphone Penetration and OS Share

Feature phones 57%

Smartphones 43%

Apple iPhone (iOS) 28%

Android 43%

RIM Blackberry 18%

Windows Mobile 7%

Other 4%

Source: Nielsen

nielsen

Data from Nielsen shows that Android is the most popular smartphone provider in North America followed by Apple. Android phones in the region account for an estimated 43%, Apple accounts for 28%, Blackberry 18% and Windows mobile 7%. Smartphone usage in the region has surpassed the 100 million mark making this the most highly penetrated smartphone market globally.

In March 2012, more than half of the mobile population in North America owned a smartphone. Although post paid subscriptions are prevalent in North America, an increasing number of mobile and smartphone users are migrating to prepaid, accounting to up to 25% of mobile phone users in the U.S alone. This trend has been largely attributed to the economic recession in the U.S., which has seen more users opt for less expensive data options.

Mobile action codes are very popular in the U.S. with 82% of them being QR (Quick Response) codes. According to Nellymoser, the average number of mobile action codes included in the top 100 U.S. magazines is 4.88 codes per issue. 35% of these codes lead users to video (see the following graphic from Nellymoser) and 21% to ecommerce. According to Austin & Williams 62% of the

U.S. consumers have scanned a QR code and 6% of the QR code scans lead to a purchase.

Video:	35%
E-Commerce:	21%
Opt-in/Subscribe/Sweeps:	20%
Social Media:	18%
Store Locator:	11%
Coupon:	8%
Photo Gallery:	7%
Downloads:	7%
Recipes:	2%
Voting:	0%

According to Forrester research, mobile commerce is projected to grow to $31 billion by 2016 in North America. This growth is precipitated by the fact that an increasing number of mobile users are willing to make purchases online using their mobile devices. This can be further attributed to increased mobile security, dynamic mobile applications that are making mobile commerce easier and websites that have been optimized for mobile. In fact, an increasing number of online retailers have a mobile strategy in place and they are leveraging the mobile usage trends in the region.

Affiliate Marketing

Geographical boundaries seem to be unimportant in affiliate marketing with up to 27% of affiliate marketers in the UK promoting North American merchants. Meanwhile up to 32% of affiliates in North America are promoting merchants in the UK.

Affiliate marketing in North America and more so in the U.S. is amongst the most flourishing globally. The practice of cost based performance is widespread in the region with many online businesses as well as brick-and-mortar enterprises rolling out affiliate networks to boost sales and to attract greater traffic to the business. Affiliate marketers in the region are as equally engaged in 'global' affiliate programs as they are with smaller local ones. ClickBank, Amazon Affiliates and Commission Junction are notably more popular in this region than anywhere in the world.

While affiliate marketing is increasingly becoming a global practice, certain attributes are unique to North America affiliate marketing trends. Affiliate marketing has gained traction in this part of the world because affiliate marketers in this region are likely to do affiliate marketing full-time. Over 50% work as full time affiliates, 31% of them own 21+ domains, 45% promote 10 merchants or less, but over 22% promote at least 80 merchants (eConsultancy). The most common marketing activities employed to promote affiliate links are: 71% use social networking sites, 30% use video and 40% use PPC advertising. The most popular sites to promote affiliate links as shown in the graphic from AffStat are Twitter (26.9%), Facebook (25%) and Linkedin (10.2%).

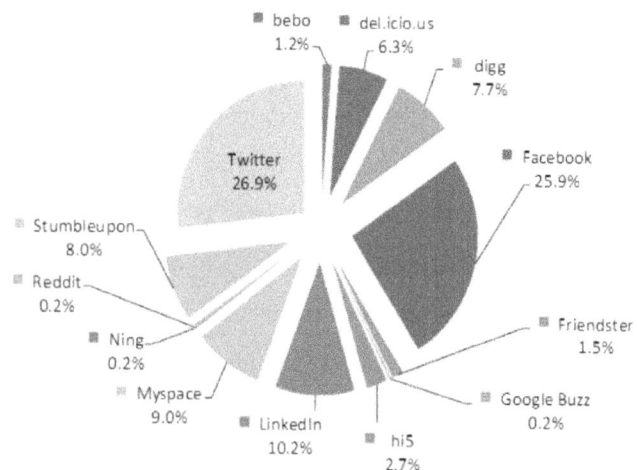

A large majority of the affiliate marketers in North America are male (72%). Of those who purchase through affiliate marketing, women represent a large majority. Health, fitness and sports industries are the most lucrative affiliate markets in the region. This is in contrast to other major affiliate markets, for example in the UK, where the travel industry is the most popular affiliate marketing segment.

While Affiliate Window is the most popular affiliate-marketing platform in the UK, Commission Junction is the most significant in North America and particularly in the U.S. Other important affiliate networks in this region are LinkShare, ShareASale and Google Affiliate Networks.

In North America, affiliates are usually engaged in business-to-business promotion. Additionally, affiliates in this region are more likely to have direct collaborations with merchants who have developed their own affiliate program.

One of the greatest challenges facing affiliates in the U.S. is the 'Amazon Tax'. This legislation allows states to impose and collect taxes from retailers who sell out of state for example Amazon.com. While this law is applicable in New York already, other states are considering following this trend. This means that the revenue generated through local websites ran by affiliates in the state is liable to taxation.

A recent report by Forrester shows the trends that affiliate marketing in North America will take in the coming two years. According to the report, smartphones and other mobile devices such as iPads, laptops and tablets are set to permeate the affiliate marketing industry in this region and to play a more considerable role. This will have a significant impact on affiliate marketers and advertisers as they have to look for new methods of leveraging mobile traffic to ensure a maximum return on investment. As affiliate marketing in the region takes a more mobile approach, affiliate marketers need to understand the sort of mobile traffic that will convert. Presently, the highest conversion rates are in downloads and video enrollments. It is also important for both local and global businesses looking to roll out affiliate networks in this region to really test which promotional channels work best with regard to mobile traffic conversion.

In addition to the growing role of mobile in affiliate marketing in North America, social media is also changing the affiliate marketing landscape in the region. With a large majority of the online population in US and Canada participating on social networks, affiliates and advertisers have the opportunity to reach out to their prospects, and to make profits in return. While Facebook, Twitter, YouTube and Flickr are significant social media platforms for affiliates in North America, Pinterest is also gaining traction in the industry.

In the backdrop of the global economic recession, an increasing number of companies are looking to increase their revenue. As such, companies in North America and especially those in the U.S. are rolling out affiliate programs in other countries for the purpose of improving their revenue streams. Meanwhile, companies outside the region are looking to expand into the region to tap into the consumer base there. Affiliate marketing offers a viable method for global businesses seeking to reach the North America consumers.

Video Marketing

Both, the U.S. and Canada host a large population of online video consumers. A report by eMarketer (2011) shows that an estimated 52% of businesses in the U.S. are using video marketing. This is a significant growth from 2009 where video marketing averaged at 39% for companies in the U.S. Additionally, comScore data indicates that an approximated 181 million Internet viewers watched an estimated 37 billion online content in just a single month.

Most online video consumers in the region engage with brand videos to learn more about a product. Most viewers in the U.S. report that they are likely to spend more time watching a video that included demonstrations of how a product works. This is an important consideration for marketers looking to tap into this market through video marketing. It is less about hard selling and more about telling the audience how a product works and how it will benefit them. It is also noteworthy that online consumers who are following a brand on social media are likely to view a video posted by that brand, according to Direct Marketing News data.

Google Sites remains the most popular video property in the U.S., attributable to YouTube viewership. It attracts up to 158 million unique visitors with 54% female viewers. Yahoo! Sites follows this, attracting an estimated 54 million unique visitors, while Vevo, Facebook and Microsoft Sites attract an estimated 50 million, 44 million and 43 million unique visitors each month. Hulu, a site that offers free TV shows and videos online is very popular amongst the 18-34 age group. Approx. 85% of U.S. Internet users watched online videos and the average video content consumer watches up to 22 hours of online video in a month.

Canadians are the most prolific online video viewers globally. However, there is a gap between this high consumption and what digital marketers are offering their audience. According to BrightRool Canada and Interactive Advertising Bureau of

Canada, marketers are not investing as much as they should in video marketing to keep up with consumers' demands. According to comScore data (2011) up to 90% of the country's online population (approximately 22.3 million) consumes online videos each month. Each viewer consumes an average of 300 videos each month. However, just 8.9% of digital marketers and companies used digital video marketing in their overall marketing campaign in that year (2011). This is in spite the fact that they believe that online videos are more effective than social networks or TV in the country.

Price considerations seem to be the biggest hindrance for video marketing in Canada. Many digital marketers are not able to track the ROI of their investment on video marketing, and as such believe that the cost of production is higher than the returned profits of this form of marketing.

Ecommerce

Admittedly, ecommerce in North America is more established than it is in most parts of the world. This can be attributed to the developed online payment infrastructure, the willingness and capability of businesses to establish online retail shops and the high Internet penetration rates in the region. However, ecommerce has made greater strides in the U.S. than it has in Canada, largely because retailers in Canada have not fully embrace the profitable potential of ecommerce.

According to Price Water Coppers Global Multi-Channel Consumer Survey (2011), up to 74% of Internet users in the U.S. shop online at least once each month. While this is a high value compared to that in other regions such as Latin America and some European countries, it is lower than rates in the UK, where up to 81% of online population shops online.

US online shoppers are generally prompted to shop by email notifications and their deliberate need to find out about a brand and its product offering. According to exacttarget.com 66% of the U.S. consumers have purchased as a result of an email and only 20% as a result of a Facebook marketing message. An estimated 55% of the online population in the country buys directly from a brand or the manufacturer.

Email	**66%**
Direct mail (letters, catalogs, postcards, etc.)	**65%**
Telephone	**24%**
Facebook	**20%**
Text messaging (SMS) on a cell phone	**16%**
Mobile App	**10%**
Twitter	**6%**
Linkedin	**4%**

In 2011, online shopping in the U.S. amounted to an estimated $162 billion, which is a 13% growth from the previous year. The most bought products are electronics, digital content such as e-books and subscriptions to web content, fashion accessories, software and children's toys. U.S. online shoppers also spend significant amount on smartphones and other mobile devices including tablets. Amazon, Ebay and other big online retailers, have popularized price-checking apps; an increasing number of online shoppers are using these apps for their shopping processes.

In the U.S., Amazon is the most popular online shopping platform. In the financial year of 2010 and 2011, Amazon US generated over $34 billion in sales. In the second quarter of 2011, the site attracted an estimated 94 million unique visitors each month. This is in contrast to another large online retailer, Target that attracted just 22 million unique visitors.

Credit cards are popular in the U.S. and many online consumers use these cards as the preferred payment method, followed by debit cards. According to data from the Federal Reserve, payments in the country are increasingly becoming electronic with more and more people opting to use credit cards, debit cards and ATM cards for their ecommerce transactions. However, the country is experiencing a decline in credit card usage in part due to the economic downturn as well as the new regulation under the Credit Card Accountability Responsibility and Disclosure Act. These regulations have made credit card usage more stringent and banks have increased interest rates on the once affordable credit cards. Prepaid cards are beginning to play a significant role for the U.S. consumer, as an alternative to credit cards and cash payments.

According to the North America B2C E-Commerce Report by yStats.com by the end of 2012, online purchases are expected to grow in both Canada and the U.S. This is underscored by the growth of mobile-commerce, which has made it easier for consumers to make transactions online.

As indicated earlier, Canadian ecommerce is still far behind the trends in the U.S. While up to 80% of the population in Canada uses Internet, a very small percentage engages in frequent online shopping. The yStats.com report attributes this to the high cost of local and cross border online shopping. The high costs locally are precipitated by the sheer lack of competition among the existing e-retailers.

However, for the marginal ecommerce, that takes place in Canada, travel, entertainment tickets, and books are the most popular items bought online.

Taxation And Border Fees

Following current legislative ruling in the U.S., over a dozen states have required online retailers to collect taxes on online purchases. This means that tax-free online shopping is likely to be a thing of the past in the U.S. as more states seek implement the regulation. Online shoppers who purchase goods abroad online are liable to the applicable U.S. tax, import duty and customs.

In Canada, import custom duties and tax are equally applicable for goods bought abroad online. However, the North American Free Trade Agreement (NAFTA) protects

Canadian consumers from paying duty on most products manufactured in America or Mexico.

However, the tax and import duty paid on goods bought/imported from other countries depends on the type of goods and the country from which they were bought. For example, luxury items imported by a consumer into Canada attract an excise duty. Generally, goods that are bought from a foreign business do not attract assessment unless custom authorities in the country collect an estimated $1 in taxes and import duty.

Alibaba

Alibaba has only just made its entry into the North American market and specifically in the U.S. The platform was launched recently and offers its services in English to cater to the audience in this region. As of March 2011, only 1.3 million US users were registered.

Alibaba presents a convenient opportunity for US retailers looking to connect directly with suppliers of cheaper raw materials and finished goods. The platform has potential for growth given the fact that it can help eliminate the bureaucracy that is often present when finding a suitable foreign supplier especially from China. Alibaba aggregates these suppliers, their products and services and makes them easily available for global trade.

However, eBay is still a very popular brand in the region, and it will pose as a great challenge to Alibaba even though the two platforms have different models. eBay caters to consumers selling or buying very specific products, while Alibaba seeks to link suppliers with wholesale businesses.

5
Online Marketing In Europe

The 62% Internet penetration in Europe has boosted global business and in particular Internet marketing and ecommerce. According to internetworldstats.com there are more than 500 million Europeans online spending an average of 15 hours weekly, with a third of them using more than one device to access Internet - 64% access Internet via a computer and 21% via a mobile (iabeurope.eu).

Country	% who go online using a computer	% who go online using a mobile
Europe Average	64%	21%
Western Europe	79%	31%
Northern Europe	86%	36%
Southern Europe	59%	19%
Central & Eastern Europe	53%	14%

Source: Mediascope Europe 2012

The Internet users in Europe have almost doubled the North American online users and represent approx. 25% of the world's Internet users. Marketers who are looking to meet their global objectives now have the infrastructure to establish online shops that carter to the multiplicity of their global audience. Europe is a diverse continent, with different languages, cultures and different degrees of technology savvy. Thus, it is essential for marketers to consider these differences as they engage with their European audience.

Cultural Differences: Do's And Dont's

Although Europeans share a continent, enjoy open borders for trade and travel and they are increasingly moving toward currency unification, each country's personality is different. Each country is likely to accommodate your marketing efforts very differently. The following is a list of the top 10 Internet countries in Europe as per internetworldstats.com.

Top 10 Internet Countries in Europe
December 31, 2011

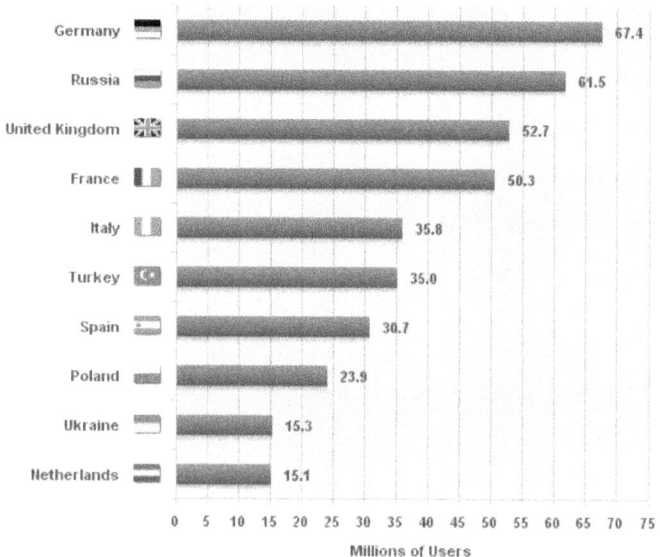

Germany ▬ 67.4
Russia ▬ 61.5
United Kingdom ▤ 52.7
France ▯ 50.3
Italy ▯ 35.8
Turkey ◀ 35.0
Spain ▤ 30.7
Poland ▬ 23.9
Ukraine ▭ 15.3
Netherlands ▭ 15.1

0   5   10   15   20   25   30   35   40   45   50   55   60   65   70   75
Millions of Users

Source: Internet World Stats - www.internetworldstats.com/stats4.htm
Basis: 500,723,686 estimated Internet Users in Europe on 2010Q4
Copyright © 2001-2012, Miniwatts Marketing Group

Germany: ranks 6th in the world for Internet usage (with 68 million online users) and has more users online than Russia or the UK.   German, as a first language is the 2nd most spoken language in Europe after Russian and above French and is the 6th most spoken language online. When browsing or shopping online, Germans are concerned about security, privacy and quality and you need to make sure that all of these are covered on your website if you plan to target this market. Also ease of online checkout and product choice are determinant factors when buying online in Germany. When searching online, 37% of Germans used one word queries, 32% two words and 25% three to four words. If you plan to use Google Analytics on your site, mention it in your privacy policy and also use an IP mask function to instruct Analytics to not save the full IP address of your visitors. For more details on this please read the post on webpronews.com.

Russia: ranks 7th in the world for Internet usage (with 62 million online users). Only 5% of the population speak English and the main financial centres are in Moscow and St Petersburg. Yandex is the search engine most used in Russia, Belarus, Ukraine and Kazakhstan. Russia leads Europe in terms of online video viewers and is followed by Germany, France, UK, Italy and Spain. A very popular social networking site there is Vkontakte (which means in 'touch') and is Facebook's rival in Russia. According to comScore there are 40 million users on VKontakte, 32 million on Odnoklassniki (which means 'Classmates') and only 4% or 12 million of the Russian online users have a Facebook account.

UK: ranks 9th in the world for Internet usage (with 53 million online users) and has a 82% Internet penetration. 48% of online UK users are on Facebook. Online grocery shopping is more popular in the UK than anywhere else in the world. The UK is the 4th largest Google+ market after the U.S., India and Brazil.

France: ranks 10th in the world for Internet usage (with 50 million online users) and has a 70% Internet penetration. French is the language spoken by 200 million people (as first and second language) in 29 countries including Canada, Switzerland, Luxembourg, Belgium, Algeria, Morocco and Tunisia to name a few. Overblog is the second most popular social networking site in France after Facebook. More than 70% of the French online users have shopped online for fashion, food and travel. If you plan to target this market bear in mind that your site needs to be translated into the local language and visuals on the site are very important. Also order tracking and product choice are determinant factors when purchasing online in France.

Italy: has a 51% Internet penetration and 36 million online users. A good-looking site is a requirement if you plan to penetrate this market as culturally, Italians are very receptive to image. PayPal and online banking are the most commonly used payment methods online. For press release submissions, I recommend checking sites such as informazione.it, notiziefresche.info and a-zeta.it. The country with the fewest online users is Vatican City with approx. 100 users.

Spain: has a 62% Internet penetration and 31 million users online. Its mobile market is one of the largest in Europe. There are four official languages in Spain: Castilian spoken by 74% of the population, Catalan spoken by 17%, Galician spoken by 7% and Basque spoken by 2%. The Spanish language is the third most spoken language online after English and Chinese and it is the official language in 22 countries. If you plan to penetrate this market remember to include customer service details and return facilities in your Terms and Conditions.

Netherlands: has a 89% Internet penetration and 15 million users online. This is a good market to target on Twitter and Linkedin as the Netherlands have more than 27% of its population on these two social networks. Other than Dutch, the Netherlands' official language, 70% of its population speak English and 60% German. Do not make the common mistake and call this country 'Holland' as North and South Holland represent only 2 of the 12 provinces that the country has and some people can take offence with this naming of their country. Some of the most popular sites in the country are: Hyves (equivalent of Facebook) and

Marktplaats.nl (equivalent of eBay). The most popular online payment methods in the Netherlands are iDeal and AcceptGiro.

One of the factors to consider when marketing to Europe is the fact that Europeans do not share their information easily, for example when compared to Americans. The Europeans are very strict about privacy and outright soliciting of information will not appeal to your target audience. In fact, there are strict regulations against soliciting information through emails, without a marketer receiving express consent from the consumer. However, privacy varies from one country to another. For example, the German market is more concerned about its privacy than the Russian market.

Marketers also need to consider the type of merchandise they can sell online to their European audience. While it may be acceptable to sell pills on the Internet in the UK, the people in Netherlands may not welcome this. It is important to find out what people are willing to buy and sell online and what they are reluctant to purchase online.

How you address your audience is also an important consideration. While in America, your audience may be more relaxed about titles and more concerned about the product or service, in Europe it is different. Be sure to officially address your audience especially when marketing to an elderly audience or a high-end market. For example, if you were marketing to a French market, you would use the term 'vous' in place of 'tu', in Germany you would use 'Sie' instead of 'Du', all meaning 'You.'

Another factor to keep in mind is how different European nationalities perceive time. For example when marketing to in the Netherlands, take into consideration that a large majority of Dutch have dinner at about six in the evening. It is unlikely you will find a large Dutch audience online at this time, more so if they have a family. It is intrusive to market to them through their mobile phones at this time too.

Additionally, you do not want to host a webinar at 8pm in France, or between 9pm and 10 pm in Spain, because it is dinnertime in these countries. In Spain and in France, their lunch times are extended, and this may not be a good time to market either. Morning times might be a better option for social media and search engine marketing.

Website Design And Customer Engagement

An important element of design when creating a multilingual site is color and graphics. These two elements will have an impact on how well your European audience accepts your brand and product offering. It is important to understand what different colors mean to different cultures and countries in Europe.

While the Asian and American audience may be attracted by extravagant graphics in websites, the Europeans tend to be more conservative. The audience here tends to look out for cleaner web pages and simple-to-use interfaces. A large majority of the European audience is also less attracted by funky logos and brand or product names. Official sounding names will be reassuring to your audience and they are more likely to take your brand seriously.

Unlike the Asian audience, which prefers serenading music in the background when they open a webpage, the European audience may not be too keen on this. Music preferences go hand in hand with attitudes to logos and brand names. If you accompany your online marketing content with music, be sure that it is inoffensive, not annoyingly loud or exceedingly funky.

Color Meanings

Red: Symbolizes passion and exhilaration in most of Western Europe. In this part of Europe, it may also have religious expressions when mixed with green, to symbolize Christmas. In Eastern Europe, red may however represent danger, power and politics, as the color is associated with communism.

Orange: Represents bounty and harvest as characterized by autumn. In most of Europe, it symbolizes warmth and fruitfulness while in countries like Netherlands it is a national color representing the national football team and the royalty.

Yellow: Is particularly loved in most European countries. It is a representation of summer, the sun and hospitability. However, yellow is symbolic of envy in Germany and may not go too well with your German audience.

Blue: Is also much used in Europe as a symbol of formality. It represents masculinity, authority, trust. However, it can also be a symbol of serenity, sobriety or depression.

Black: is equally considered symbolic of power and formality and depending on the context, death.

Other factors to take into consideration when designing your website for the European audience are:

Europeans do not give out their personal information and profiles easily. Come up with ways that will encourage them to offer information that is helpful for your online marketing campaign. For example, you can get your audience involved in a pro-European initiative.

The audience in Europe undertakes extensive research before purchasing or subscribing to anything. Be sure to make it easy for them to find information by offering adequate content on your website.

Europeans are particular about giving you their time. Thus, include social widgets or applications that are beneficial to them and will help them to meet their needs.

Europeans, especially the young, the tech savvy and the high-end are on the lookout for relevant and up-to-date information. Keep your website updated with relevant news and content.

Because Europeans (especially the British, Russians, Swedes and Germans) use social media to research before buying a product, testimonials are very important to them. As such, almost half of the audiences in Europe who use social media use it for search, particularly to find product recommendations.

Websites are also required to comply with the European Union E-Privacy policies. These laws, which became effective at the start of 2011, prevent webmasters and marketers from using consumer information that they find online for example from social media profiles, without the consumers' consent. If you are using any tracking technology including cookies on your website, you need to inform site visitors that their information may be tracked. You also need to tell site visitors why tracking is required as well as obtain their express permission. The consent you receive from a site visitor may be in the form of them clicking an icon or a link. The only form of user tracking exempted from this policy is the type that is essential to providing a service to the consumer. These include online applications, side caching to boost page performance and speed, and online shopping carts. However, you are not exempted if you are advertising or using analytical tools (e.g. Google Analytics and custom greetings) as part of your marketing strategy. This policy is further applicable even for

European businesses that host their business websites overseas.

To comply with these directives, it is advisable that you eliminate non-essential cookies and find creative ways to obtain users' permission to track and use their information.

Search Engine Marketing (SEO & PPC)

For most marketers, the main concern in optimizing a website for a European audience is the language barriers. There are fifty countries in Europe and it can certainly be a mammoth task to try to optimize a site for all these languages. An important first step to take is to consider working with a European SEO firm that will help you with correct translation and targeted optimization. Alternatively get a native to create content for your site. It is important that you select domains and write each site for every targeted country in Europe.

While optimizing for Europe may seem like a challenging task, it is well worthwhile. Europeans are very active web searchers; there are more than 500 million online potential clients to tap into if you do your optimization right.

Your SEO strategy for Europe must take into consideration the local search engines in each country that you plan to target. Optimizing your multilingual site for the local search engines can go a long way to improve your market share in the continent. Some of the most popular local search engine sites include:

Google: is still the most dominant search engine in Europe. More than 60% of Europeans spend a significant amount of time online and more than half of this population searches with Google. However, Google's dominance in Europe is facing stiff competition from alternative search engines.

Bing: although Google is a large player in the UK and in the French market, Bing is increasingly taking up a large market share. Today, approximately 4% of the search population in the UK uses Bing as an alternative to Google. An additional advantage is the collaboration between Yahoo and Bing, whose search results account for 4% of the UK and about 2.8% in France. For marketers, optimizing your site for Bing in Europe can have significant return on investment. However, in most European countries Bing is simply Live Search with the Bing brand logo. As such, optimizing for Bing in the UK doesn't mean you have optimized adequately for Bing in Austria, for example.

Yandex: is the most popular search engine in Eastern Europe and specifically in Russia. In Russia, Yandex has outdone Google as the preferred search engine, accounting for 64% of the search market. If you are looking to do business in Russia, then you must optimize your site for Yandex search. This search engine has the capacity to determine search engine infractions; as such, you are able to precisely understand the search behavior of Russian online users. It is important that you pay attention to the keywords and how users are likely to use these keywords in their search. If possible, use the services of a Russian native speaker to get the language and keyword formation right. Recently, Yandex launched an English-based search engine.

Seznam: is the most dominant search engine in the Czech Republic. The search engine was initially developed as a web portal but presently it is a full-scale search engine. In Czech, Seznam has a greater market share when compared to Google, in terms of search. Although the Czech Republic is not the largest market in Europe, it is certainly one of the most active.

Conduit and T-online: T-online is the largest search engine in Germany after Google. In essence, it is a portal powered by the Google search. Thus, it is not entirely a different optimization option from Google. On the other hand, there is Conduit, which has a larger market in Germany when compared to Yahoo or Bing. In Spain, Conduit accounts for 2.9% of the search market.

Vinden.nl: 95% of the share market in Netherlands uses Google as the preferred search engine. However, the search engine users as well as marketers have not overlooked the importance of Vinden, which accounts for up to 3% of the search market. This search engine is partially powered by Google search engine too.

These are just a few search engines used in some of the largest and active markets in Europe. There are other alternatives in each country including Onet.pl in Poland, Orange in France and Ask.com in the Nordic region and in the UK.

In most of Europe, marketers continue to use search marketing even though businesses are cutting down on their operational and advertising budgets. Studies by eMarketer and the European Interactive Advertising Association indicate that online marketing is set to grow across the country in the coming years. There are up to 178 million people coming online each week in Europe, thus the search market is very lucrative in the continent. Most marketers in Europe are in fact focusing most of their efforts on both organic and paid search marketing, more than they are traditional avenues of marketing and advertising.

Another study undertaken by research firm Forrester Research shows that marketers in Europe are likely to spend up to 3 billion Euros on paid search marketing in the years between 2004 and 2012. The largest markets in terms of search marketing expenditure are the UK and Germany. Marketers in the finance, retail, auto and travel niches are spending the most on sponsored links and paid advertisements for traffic generation.

Presently in Europe, paid search has a lower cost-per-click spend especially in local search engines; the market is yet to reach its full capacity when compared to the U.S. market. The rate of cost-per-click will certainly rise as more and more marketers focus their marketing efforts in paid search to generate traffic. However, this will not happen at once in all European markets and the costs of paid search are likely to escalate in larger and more active markets.

As you undertake paid search with an eye for the Europe market, be sure to take into consideration the different regions and languages. Your campaign should be structured to optimize keywords according to language inflections and local search engines. In addition to optimizing your keywords for local search, do the same for your sites' landing pages; these need to be locally optimized for a successful search engine marketing campaign.

Search engine marketing in Europe will work best when you pay attention to the local target market. Adapting to local search engines will allow you to determine the users' intent, thereby understanding how to meet their needs. Thus, if you are looking to market your brand and product offering in Europe, you must not approach the continent as a single target market. The bottom line is that SEM in Europe is largely language centric. Other factors that influence search engine marketing in this market include culture, perceptions, legal policies, and regional values. Given the increasingly active online population in Europe, it is possible to attract up to 1 million monthly site visitors even in smaller countries.

Social Media Marketing

According to a study by the research group Ecircles, 37% of Twitter users and up to 27% of Facebook users in some European countries (UK, France, Germany, Italy and Netherlands) use these networks to find out about products and brands. The study also shows that marketers can reach up to 56% of their target market using email marketing as well as social media marketing. Admittedly, a large share of the European market is not inclined to share information they find on social media networks with their friends on the same platforms. This is a contrast when compared to the American market, where sharing with your network is an essential aspect of social media.

While marketers reaching out to an American audience, for example, may be realistically looking for a viral effect, the Ecircle study shows that the viral effect is not among the priorities for social media marketers in Europe. As such, as you market to the European market using social media, you must give your audience a very compelling reason why they should share your message or spread the word about your product offering and brand.

An InSites Consulting survey shows that up to 73 % (almost 347 million users) of Internet users in Europe utilize social networks. Facebook is the most popular social media site in a large majority of the countries in Europe, accounting for an estimated 62% of social media users.

While 80% of Europeans are familiar with Twitter, only 16% of them actively engage with this platform. However, 28% of non-Twitter users say they intend to start using the site soon. Twitter users in Europe are mostly men and come from active online markets including UK and Germany. The highest Facebook penetration in Europe comes from countries such as: Monaco (95%), Iceland (70%), Gibraltar (69%), UK (60%) and Norway (57%) while the countries with the highest number of Facebook accounts in Europe are: UK (37 million), France (24.5 million), Germany (24 million) and Italy (22 million) (socialbakers.com).

In Eastern Europe, Vkontakte comes third after Twitter, accounting for an estimated 12% of the social media market share. Linkedin comes fourth accounting for up to 11% between both Eastern and Western European countries. Surprisingly, Eastern European countries and those in the South are more active social media users than users in Western European countries.

In Russia, Vkontakte shares a close similarity with Facebook usage, and it is in fact considered the Facebook of Russia and Eastern Europe. Vkontakte is number 42 out of 500 in the most popular social networking site in the world. There are over 135 million users on this platform all across Eastern Europe.

In France, Skyrock is the most popular social network but many of its users continue to diverge to Facebook. There are up to 23 million Skyrock users in France, but 30% of these users still engage with Facebook as an alternative social network.

In Spain, Tuenti was the most popular social networking platform, until Facebook took a stronghold in this market. There are up to 11 million Facebook users in Spain and about 7 million Tuenti users.

In Germany, StudiVZ Groups is the most used social media network with up to 15 million users. However, some of these users also utilize other social networking platforms including Facebook and Twitter.

In Netherlands, a large majority of its population is loyal to its local social networking site Hyves. This platform has double the number of Facebook users in the country.

Different regions in Europe have different uses for social media. For example, in Italy social media is largely used in the education sector while in the UK and Germany, online users utilize social media for undertaking research before making a purchase or for work purposes. Russians use social media to link up with friends, to share content and to find new contacts. Spain's online community is also actively engaged in making new connections and sharing content across the platforms. One would expect countries such as UK, Germany or the Netherlands to be some of the most active social media users, but these markets are generally conservative when it comes to social media.

For a majority of Europeans, price remains a main factor when making a purchasing decision. A large percentage of online users thus resort to social media sites before they can finally decide to buy a product. Studies by Ecommerce Europe show that Germans are loyal to a brand that they already know and may be reluctant to give in to social media reviews and online advertising. On the contrary, the Spaniards and Poles shop around and they use social media to compare prices and learn more about a new product or brand. 60% of the British and French are as conservative as the Germans in terms of shopping around using online tools such social media.

Email Marketing

Email marketing in Europe is distinctively different from what it is in America. In countries like the U.S., email marketing is only seen as effective when a marketer builds a list of over 5,000 leads and existing customers. Anything below this is not considered to generate a justifiable return on investment. However, in Europe email-marketing lists are considerably smaller. This makes micro segmenting your audience for better targeting less cost effective. However, this does not mean that email marketers in Europe do not segment their audience, especially based on loyalty.

In Europe, marketers are increasingly using email marketing in combination with social media to find leads and to engage with existing clients. This is especially important because as indicated earlier, a large majority of social media users in Europe use social media to make purchasing decisions.

According to an Ecircle study, a large majority of online users in Spain, Italy and UK access their emails through mobile phones at least once every day. If you are looking to target these markets, consider establishing a mobile friendly email campaign.

The online markets in Germany, Netherlands and Italy demonstrate more willingness to subscribe to newsletters. Meanwhile the markets in Spain and UK are less inclined to subscribe to newsletters. This is an important consideration to take in both your list building strategies and customer retention campaigns. Newsletters are essential features for lead generation and for engaging with your existing clients.

In Europe, an estimate 75% of marketers use direct email marketing, which entails sending newsletters to an individual's address. Additionally email marketing as a means of customer and sales generation is more popular in the UK. In contrast, just half of the studied marketers in Italy use email marketing.

As indicated earlier, emails that are targeted toward specific segments work best in Europe. However, marketers can struggle to segment their typically small lists. Additionally a good number of European marketers use multi-level email marketing even though it is not as efficient.

For the European marketer, the main goals of an email marketing campaign are to boost brand awareness, promote a new product offering and to improve customer loyalty.

Email marketing in Europe is regulated by the Privacy and Electronic Communications policy issued by the European Union in 2002. The EU policies do not have any practical enforcement; each country implements the law within the structure of their own legal system. While there may not be any way for local jurisdictions to enforce the law against foreign transgressors, it is important that you comply to avoid future complications. According to the EU directives:

a) Marketers can only send marketing emails to recipients who opt-in through subscription or another form of express consent.

b) If a marketer has an existing client who has not refused to be contacted and marketed to through email, the marketer may continue to market his products and service to this client. However, you must make it easy for the client to opt-out when he desires to.

c) You may send commercial messages such advertisements to other businesses or employees of a certain firm without their consent. However, you must make it free and easy for them to opt-out of your emails.

d) The email-marketing directive disallows you to hide your identity when sending marketing emails. You must also include an address that enables the recipient to notify you when they want to opt-out.

Mobile Marketing

Mobile marketing in Europe, as in other parts of the world is increasingly popular due to the high penetration of mobile phones and the growing trends. Marketers are turning to mobile marketing because more and more people are using mobile devices to check email, engage in social networks, shop and find businesses that offer great deals.

More than 80% of mobile phone users in the UK, France and Germany use their phones to access news and work based information. On the contrary, a majority of users in other countries in Europe use mobile devices for social media engagement. According to a comScore study, up to 42% of European iPhone users use their mobile device to access a social networking site. Also up to 70% of iPhone users accessed their emails through their mobile devices while only 26% of non-iPhone smartphone users checked and sent email using their mobile devices.

The tops European countries in terms of smartphone adoption are Norway and Sweden with more than half of their population having a smartphone (Our Mobile Planet).

Smartphone Penetration

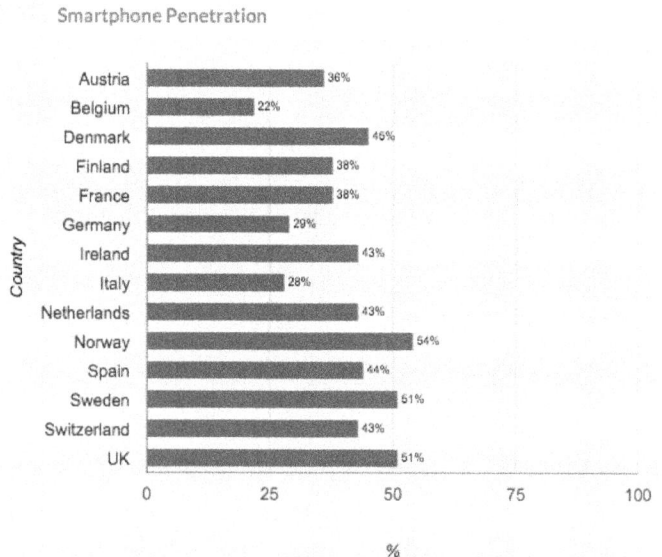

The iPhone is the most preferred Operating System in Europe (Our Mobile Planet).

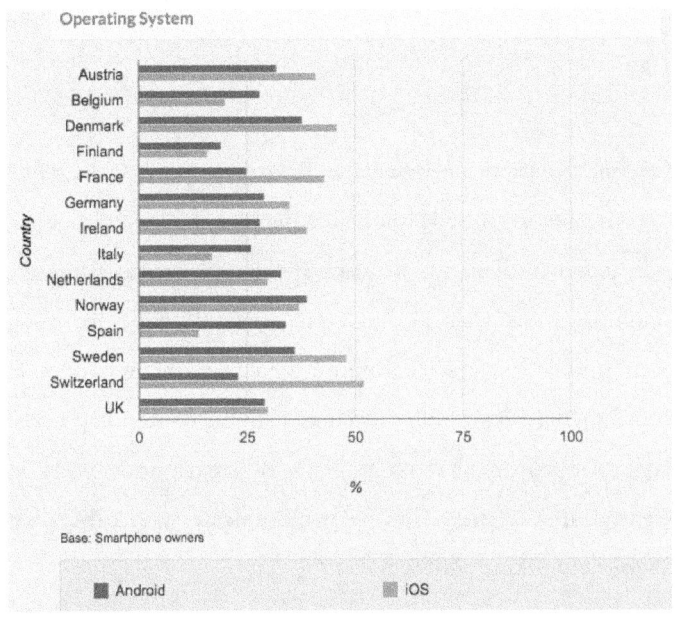

Other studies by comScore show that most men in Europe use smartphones than they do regular cell phones; for example in the UK up to 75% of iPhone users are male while in France up to 67% percent. comScore data shows that iPhone 3G network capability will increase iPhone usage and pose a stiff competition across Europe. The 3G penetration in the UK is at approximately 26%, while in Germany and France it is at about 23% and 17% respectively.

In terms of action mobile codes usage such as QR codes, Germany comes second after the U.S. and leads Europe according to an article on internetretailing.net. 24% of Germans have used QR codes compared to only 12% in the UK.

Overall, smartphone owners in Europe present a lucrative opportunity for mobile marketers because it is easier to reach this audience than it is to reach those with standard mobile phones. Most smartphone users across Europe are using their mobile devices for Internet banking, online shopping, social media networking as well as a source of trending news. It is noteworthy that up to 75% of smartphone users in Central and Eastern Europe communicate with others via social networking platforms.

In terms of short message usage, European countries tend to lag behind. While Americans are sending over 600 messages each month per mobile phone user, users in European countries especially in the Nordic regions are sending just 150 messages per month. SMS pricing in Europe plays a large role as most European countries price their SMS services at about 10 cents per message. This is much higher than the cost of messaging in Asia and in the U.S. These pricing trends have driven mobile phone users to seek alternatives for instant messaging, with the most immediate being popular social networking platforms.

A large majority of mobile phone users are on prepaid services. According to a report by the Federal Communications Commission up to 60% of European mobile phone users are on prepaid services compared to just 11% of users in the U.S.

According to a comScore study, in the UK, Germany, France, Italy and Spain, mobile marketers reach up to 100 million subscribers through SMS advertisements. However, the same study shows that only half of that population actually saw the advertisement on their mobile phone. Yet, a larger percentage of smart phone users recall seeing the ads they subscribed to either through the web or through a mobile application. In the past two years, SMS ad penetration reached 44% of the 230 million users of mobile phones in the region.

Smartphone users across Europe use their mobile devices variously when it comes to mobile commerce. About 22% of users use their phones to take product pictures, 10% send these picture to their network, about 15% use their phones to text or call their friends to tell them about a product, 11%

use their phones to scan a retail bar code, 7% use their phones to locate a store, 6.4% make price comparisons, 4.5% research a product, 4% use their phones to find local deals.

According to Our Mobile Planet Ireland, Denmark and the UK are the top online shoppers via a mobile device.

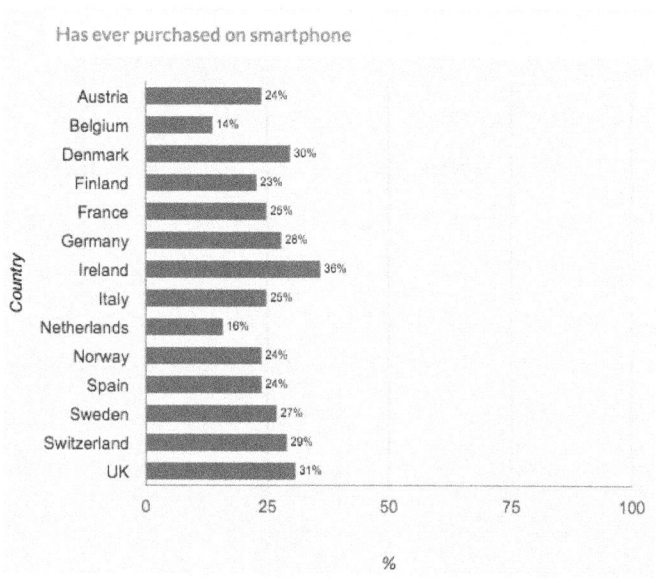

Has ever purchased on smartphone

Affiliate Marketing

When compared to the American market, the European affiliate market is still maturing. Foreign businesses looking to create an affiliate program may face challenges in generating high quality traffic. This is because Europeans are more inclined to local initiatives.

According to a report from affiliates4U.com, 80% of the European affiliates are male, 25% plans to expand their activity to Germany, CPA (cost-per-acquisition) is the most preferred payment model and SEO is the most popular way to drive affiliate traffic to sites.

Figure 17: How do you generate the majority of traffic to your website?

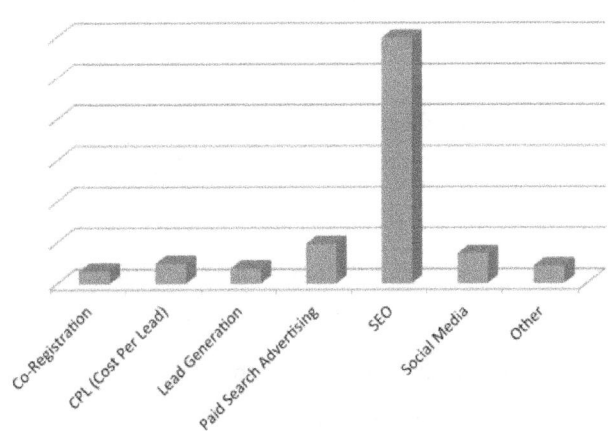

TradeDoubler is the most preferred European affiliate network (24.22%) followed by WebGains (19.25%) and Zanox (16.27%).

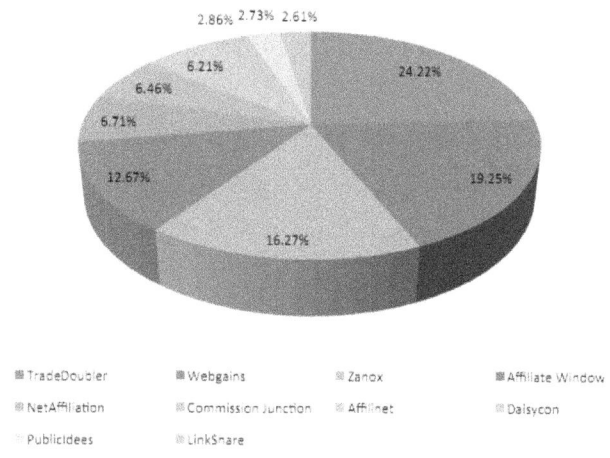

In addition, while there are more extensive affiliate networks in countries such as the U.S., the affiliate programs in Europe tend to be smaller and more localized. This is largely due to the language, cultural and regional segmentation that is characteristic of Europe. However, with the appropriate partners who understand the specific markets, it is possible to roll out a successful affiliate network.

In addition to participating in local affiliate networks, Europeans are also more inclined to participate in more established worldwide networks including ClickBank, Commission Junction, Affiliate Windows and Amazon. These established networks are popular because they are better known and trusted among the European affiliate partners market. For example, according to ClickBank, up to 18 % of its annual sales revenues and business came from Europe in 2011.

What makes an affiliate platform such as ClickBank attractive for the European market is that it is localized for the diverse languages. For example, in the past year, product sales for order forms filled in German, French and Spanish have increased by 23%, 24% and 156% respectively.

Another popular affiliate network across Europe is TradeDoubler whose market share extends to the UK, Eastern Europe, the Nordic countries as well as a large part of Western Europe.

How can you best leverage the affiliate network market in Europe?

Consider collaborating with larger networks in Europe instead of dealing directly or exclusively with foreign affiliates. Select a network that understands your goals and one that will help you to better understand the European market.

First start with a single country, optimize your platform and purchase adequate traffic. This will allow you to understand how the market in Europe works before committing to a large budget.

Video Marketing

Video marketing entails the use of videos to advertise and to attract traffic to a site. Online video advertising and marketing is a growing phenomenon. This can be attributed to the ease of creating video content and the accessibility to video sharing platforms that have made it easier for marketers to engage with their audiences.

According to comScore the largest market for online video ads is the UK. More than 22 million online users in the UK came across video ads during their online experience, up to 33 million online users searched for and watched a video ad. The male population engages more with video content, representing about 75% of online users compared to just 25% of females.

According to Our Mobile Planet, 22% of the smartphone owners in Ireland and Spain watch videos on their phones daily.

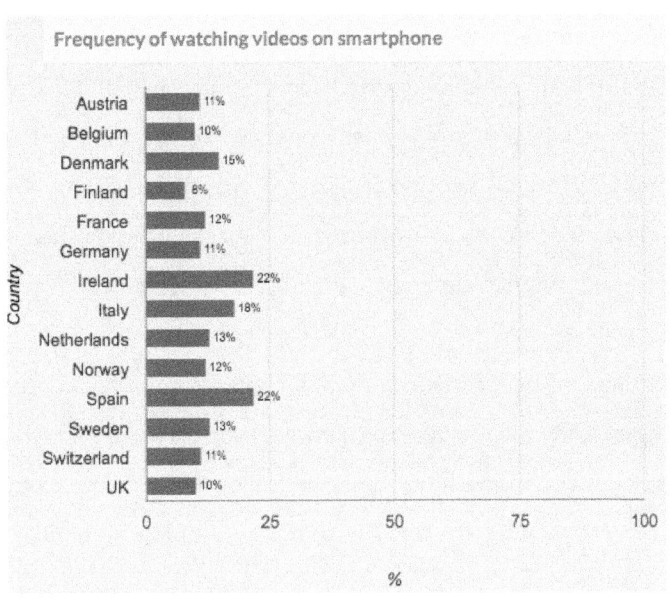

Frequency of watching videos on smartphone

Country	%
Austria	11%
Belgium	10%
Denmark	15%
Finland	8%
France	12%
Germany	11%
Ireland	22%
Italy	18%
Netherlands	13%
Norway	12%
Spain	22%
Sweden	13%
Switzerland	11%
UK	10%

The growing audience for video ads and content is largely because of advanced broadband connections as well as increased ownership of laptops among the younger generation in the region. In particular, short videos in the form of YouTube ads are more popular across Europe, with an estimated 10% of Internet users in the region watching full-length online videos.

Ecommerce

A growing number of Europeans are shopping online, not just from local brands but also from foreign sites. Studies by the European Union Statistics Agency show that up to 43%

of consumers in all the 27 EU countries aged between 16 and 74 years purchased merchandise online in 2011. The figure is however lower when compared to the U.S. online shopping trends which account for an estimated 53% of online user activity. Also approx. 10% of the EU population has used Internet to purchase in another European country.

Markets in the UK, Sweden and Denmark are more actively engaged in online shopping and account each for 71% of their online population (see the following graphic from Eurostat showing the top EU countries in online shopping). These countries are followed by Netherlands at about 67% of its population, Luxembourg at about 65%, Germany at about 64%, Finland at about 62%, and France at about 53%. There is also potential for global ecommerce in less dominant markets including Romania, Italy and Bulgaria where ecommerce is still lower compared to the continental averages.

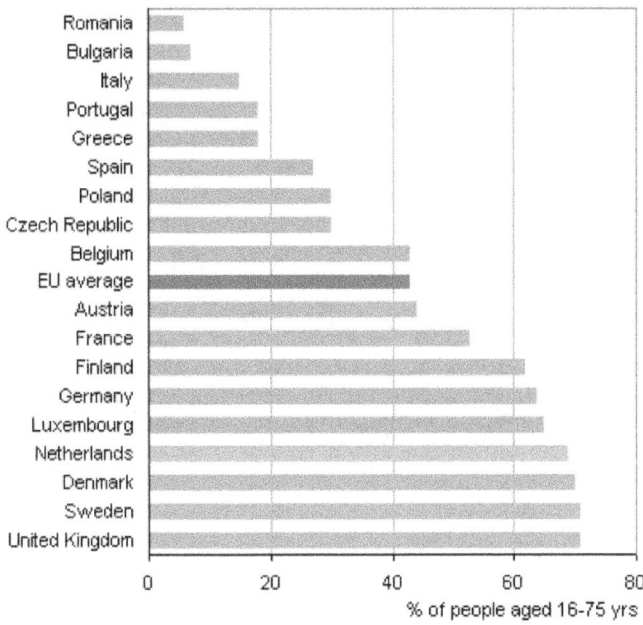

Source: Eurostat

Further analysis shows that up to 41% of the online users in Britain shopped for clothes on the Internet in 2011. This is double the regional average, which stands at 22%. In Germany, online clothing shoppers accounted for 39% of online users while in Finland and Denmark the figure is much lower at 36%. Meanwhile, in online grocery sales and food items, the UK shows higher figures at 19% while the average in Europe for online grocery sales is 6%.

Eurostat observes that by 2013 up to 50% of Europeans will be engaged in regional and global online shopping. However, international and local businesses will continue to face various barriers as they seek to penetrate the European online market. Some of these challenges include the different ecommerce laws in each country in the region as well as the payment logistics, due to the lack of uniformity in currency. Currently 17 members of the EU use the Euro: Germany, France, Belgium, Luxembourg, Finland, Ireland, The Netherlands, Italy, Estonia, Slovakia, Slovenia, Andorra, Greece, Cyprus, Austria, Malta and Portugal. The 10 countries that do not use the Euro are: UK, Denmark, Sweden, Poland, Latvia, Hungary, Romania, Bulgaria, Czech Republic, and Lithuania.

Another barrier for online global business in Europe is the language and cultural differences in each country. This can pose a big challenge for advertisers who are looking to penetrate as many markets, while remaining culturally relevant and sensitive. Each country may require a different approach to advertising and marketing and this can mean a large advertising budget for smaller businesses.

SEO challenges also remain a barrier to global ecommerce. Google has domains that are specific to each country; this means that a high ranking in one top-level domain does not necessarily translate to equally high rankings for local domain in each of your target market. Overall, a foreign business conducting ecommerce in Europe would have to create and maintain multilingual sites, plan a language specific SEO campaign and conduct various marketing and advertising campaigns for each country.

Additionally, the broadband penetration rates differ from one country to another. According to the OECD, the broadband subscription rate in Denmark and Netherlands is 37%. In Germany, the UK, Switzerland, France and Norway the penetration is about 30%. Countries in Eastern Europe including Poland and the Czech Republic have lower penetration rates of about 10%.

Some of the largest online sites include Amazon, which accounts for approximately 118 million visitors and Apple that attracts up to 53 million unique visitors. In Germany, online retailer Otto Gruppe comes in third with 33 million unique visitors.

Alibaba, a web based service that connects suppliers with buyers globally, is rapidly establishing itself in Europe and specifically in the UK. This is China's largest online trading platform and it is looking to establish itself in the vibrant ecommerce landscape in the UK.

The economic recession across Europe has narrowed the retail markets in the region. European countries such as the UK are now looking for opportunities to penetrate the booming Asian market. A platform such as Alibaba offers this opportunity. Some of the most popular British merchandise sold on Alibaba includes food and soft drinks, household furniture and agricultural products.

In Europe, different countries prefer different online payment methods. It is important to avail the appropriate payment method to guarantee a better shopping experience for your site visitors.

The Single Euro Payment Initiative played a significant role in harmonizing methods of online payment in Europe. However, the cultural differences in each country have significant impact on the preferred methods of making online payments.

Germans prefer hard copy invoices to accompany the goods they purchase. They would rather pay using their debit cards or make physical payments than use credit cards.

In Italy the inclination is toward local payment services rather than international or foreign ones such as PayPal. The most commonly used online payment services in Italy are Cartasi and Sella. The Dutch and French also seem to prefer local payment services with iDeal and e-Cart Bleue.

In the UK, online shoppers tend to use their debit cards with Visa, Maestro and MasterCard being the most popular online payment methods. The UK market has also embraced international payment methods including WorldPay and PayPal.

Border fees or taxes paid when buying online from abroad: Internet purchases made within the EU are subjected to sales taxes. Each member state in the EU has a different value added tax rate for goods purchased online and these can range between 15% and 25% of the price of the purchased item.

If you are a small business selling goods online to a European market, you can charge the applicable VAT rates in your country up to a certain level. Above this level, the VAT rate for the European client becomes applicable. Online retailers are required to register in each country they carter to and to pay VAT to the country's authority.

6
Online Marketing In Asia

Economic development and globalization have thrust countries in the Asian continent to the forefront to become some of the most lucrative markets today. Asia has the biggest number of Internet users in the world with 1 billion online users, which is double the number of Internet users in Europe and 4 times more than in North America. The growing Internet penetration (26% compared to 62% in Europe and 79% in North America) has offered the infrastructure that businesses from the West require to reach out to the attractive Asian market.

In spite of the immense opportunity that the Asian market offers, global businesses will still be faced with a couple of challenges before critical issues are streamlined. Asia, unlike the U.S. is a complex and diverse continent with different cultures, preferences and needs. Marketing to such a fragmented market can be challenging. Adopting a similar approach for each country approach will not be successful for any business seeking to penetrate the Asian market.

Cultural Differences: Dos And Don'ts

Asian culture is significantly different from the mode of operation in the West. Like in any other part of the world, it is important to understand what to do and what to avoid when doing business in Asia. The following is a list of the top ten Internet countries in Asia as per internetworldstats.com.

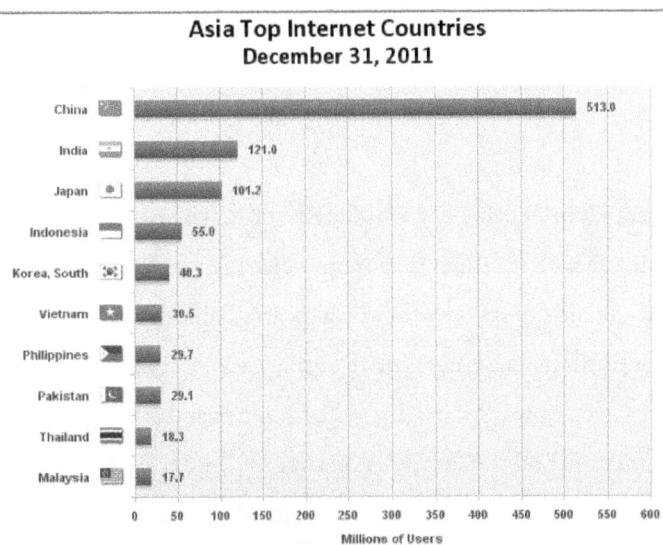

Asia Top Internet Countries
December 31, 2011

China 513.0
India 121.0
Japan 101.2
Indonesia 55.0
Korea, South 40.3
Vietnam 30.5
Philippines 29.7
Pakistan 29.1
Thailand 18.3
Malaysia 17.7

Millions of Users

China: is the country with the highest number of Internet users (513 million), which means that 1 out of every 5 persons around the world who goes online is from China.

10 million new users are joining each month and more than half of the Chinese Internet users spend 3 hours daily on the Internet. The Internet penetration in China is close to 40% while in Honk Kong is up to 70% and has approx. 5 million Internet users. The highest penetration in China comes from places such as Beijing (70%), Shanghai (66%) and Guangdong (60%). Chinese or the 'Simplified Chinese' is the most used language online after English. The most popular online shopping categories in China are: clothes, shoes, books, gifts and beer. One third of the online shoppers use debit cards to pay online, however as the daily limit for the debit cards is set at 300 RMS ($44) most of the people prefer to pay with cash or a check on delivery. Mobile web in China is more popular than in the U.S. Some of the most popular sites in China are: Baidu (search engine), QQ (instant messaging platform in Asia), Taobao (the Ebay of China), Sina Weibo (hybrid of Twitter and Facebook) and Youku Toudu (China's YouTube). More than 96% of people educated to college level and above in China use the Internet. More than 70% of the Chinese Internet users go online via their mobile device. Chinese spend 70% of leisure time online (resonancechina.com). 47% of domain names in China are .com. Instant messaging is China's top Internet activity (CNNIC). Twitter is blocked in China, however

almost 1 million people still visit it every month (We Are Social). Tianji (China's Linkedin) has 8 million users.

India: has the 3rd largest Internet population after China and the U.S. with more than 121 million users. The penetration rate in India is very low. Only 10% of the Indian population is online. 76% of the online users are under 34 years old and 70% of them are women. Indians spend the least amount of time online of any Asian nation with 11 hours per month (ADMA). 54% of the Indian population are mobile subscribers, however only 1% went online on their mobile device. Mobile usage in India exceeds desktop usage. To show the online shopping potential that India has, in 2012 Amazon launched a shopping online site and branded it junglee.com. Coupon and deal sites are very popular in India: Snapdeal, Dealsand You, Mydala and Groupon. 41% of the India online users are checking frequently education sites. Google is the first search engine with 98% reach. 8 out 10 of all Internet users are using social networking sites such as Facebook, Orkut and Google+. India is the 2nd largest market for Google+ after the U.S. There are 24 official languages in India (Hindi is spoken by 30% of the population), however the preferred medium for browsing the Internet is English. A good market to target is the Indians outside the country (more than 25 million) and they could be reached by advertising on Indian online news and entertainment sites as 'the heart of an Indian living abroad is never far from his homeland'.

Japan: has more than 100 million Internet users (78% Internet penetration) and is the 4th largest online market worldwide after China, the U.S. and India. Japanese is also the 4th most spoken language online. There are 126 monthly searches per user (how to do things, how to fill up spare time, research work and shopping research). The most popular social networks are: Mixi (in 2011 Twitter partnered with this social network to develop business and advertising opportunities), Gree (social/mobile gaming), FC2 (blog site) and Facebook. The Japanese watch more videos online than any other nations. Google is the main search engine and provides results for Yahoo! Japan and Rakuten as well. Only 25% of the Japanese businesses have their own websites (jimdo.com). Reading news online is Japan's top Internet activity.

South Korea: has 81% Internet penetration (the highest in Asia) with 40 million online users. 100% of South Koreans under 30 are online. Korean is the 10th language on the web. South Korea has the fastest Internet connection in the world. 40% of the South Korean web users have their own blogs. The top sites in South Korea are: Naver (search engine), Daum (search engine), Nate (search engine), Cyworld (Facebook's rival) and Yahoo.

In Asia, hierarchy is very important. The adults and elderly are largely in charge of decision-making. Thus, marketers would naturally look to this group, to influence others to make purchases. Overlooking the adult or elderly population and their influence will be perceived as ignorance of the structural hierarchy in the society.

When selling to the Asian market, you need to avoid 'loss of face'. This means that you should steer off any selling points or situations that are likely to embarrass you or your audience. This also ties in with the issues of hierarchy and reputation. Thus, in your marketing campaign avoid using terms that will demean any of your audience or using terms that can embarrass a certain target group or stir controversy in the society. Many Asian countries, especially China, will generally appreciate a marketing campaign or message that praises their history and traditional values. A company that takes this approach is likely to have acceptance easily.

In countries such as India, Malaysia and Indonesia religion plays an important role. Religion is thus likely to influence the approach you take in your marketing campaign. In these countries, it is best to avoid motivational selling and instead sell from the point of view of education, information and appeal to emotion.

Unlike the Western culture of wanting to get straight to the point in business, Asians prefer to build a relationship first. Trust is important for the Asian market and a business would have to establish rapport with its audience before they can even begin to engage with you. While this may be true in most other markets, in Asia a marketer would have to go an extra mile to establish a trustworthy relationship before people can enter into any business agreement or make decisions about your product.

It is important to understand how the people in Asia communicate and what their expressions mean. Your audience is unlikely to tell you 'no' even if they are not interested in a product or do not fully understand your message. Instead, they may tell you 'we will consider' or 'it is not convenient in the moment'. Instead of demanding for a 'yes' or 'no' answer, ask your audience whether they agree or disagree. Additionally, calmness and sobriety is much appreciated as opposed to loudness when sending out your message.

Website Design And Customer Engagement

Generally, countries in the West are Low Context cultures (individualistic and action-oriented cultures where words are more important than context) as opposed to countries in Asia. In Asia, culture and tradition influence just about every aspect of life including business. When designing your website for the Asian market you need to take into consideration the cultural and traditional contexts that underlie communication in these countries.

For example in China, Japan and India communication is generally indirect. The audience tends to focus on the larger meaning in communication, instead of what is being said. What does this mean for website design considerations? This means that the high context cultures that characterize the Asian market need more information on website landing pages. A website for the Asian audience will typically offer information about your brand and the history of your company, instead of getting to issues about products and prices. Remember that the Asians are looking for context and for a relationship before you can tell them about your product offering.

In addition to in depth brand information, the Asian audience will appreciate plenty of animations that are brightly colored and splashed all over the pages. Admittedly, from a Western point of view, the Asian website layout is cluttered. The Asian audience prefers communication via visual effects. Large companies such as McDonalds, Nike and Coca-Cola have designed their websites to target the Asian audience's appeal to graphics, sound and bright colors. This is in contrast to the Coca Cola website for the U.S. audience, which has a simple interface with just a single image, a single menu and a couple of links to other web pages. The Coca Cola website for the Korean audience is saturated with images of walking coke bottles and others jumping across the screen and a lot of text accompanies the images.

It is also a good idea to include many relevant links in a website created for the Asian market. Due to the emphasis on graphics and images, the Asian website will have more pages to fully cover the brand, the product offering and prices as well as pages dedicated to articles.

Another factor to take into consideration is how you set up the site's navigation. Websites for the Asian market tend to utilize parallel site navigation in contrast to the linear navigation in the West. As such, Asian web users prefer a navigation system that will open a different window each time the user opens a new page in a website. Of course, such navigation would irritate a Western web user. Also, consider using pop-ups in your website for the Asian market even though these are generally frowned upon in the West.

Websites saturated with color are much preferred in Asia. However, it is important to strategically use the colors because colors do have messages of their own. In the West, red may be symbolic of danger but in Asia, and specifically in China it is the color of good luck and celebration. In India, red is associated with purity.

You might want to avoid splurging your website with green for a Chinese audience. Green is associated with infidelity and mistrust. Additionally, while white may be symbolic of peace and purity in the West, for many in Asia it is associated with death and sadness. A safe color to use for the Asian website is blue, which is generally viewed as a neutral color.

As you develop a website for the Asian market, it is advisable that you purchase independent top-level domains for every country that you are looking to reach (for example, .kr for Korea and .jp for Japan). Be sure that servers in the specific country host the domains to assist with local search engine rankings in that country. If this approach of buying different top-level domains for each county is costly and cumbersome to set up, consider buying one top-level domain and then setting up sub-domains for each target country or language.

A website is a great platform for collecting site visitors and target audience information. However, the Asian audience is very wary of spam given that spamming is a significant concern in Asia. As such, users may be hesitant to give out their information.

Nevertheless, the Asian market is typically appreciative of a company that creates a platform for discussion and exchange of information. A study by Global Web Index showed that up to 64% of web users in Asia share their opinion online through a blog, forums, emails and instant messaging. The market in Asia is keen on discussing about brands on online platforms. In addition to sharing information, they also use these platforms to seek recommendations before purchasing. In fact, Global Web Index shows that over a third of the participating web users read customer reviews and sought recommendations from online contacts before making a purchase decision.

What does this mean for your marketing efforts? It means that the Asian audience will appreciate a website that offers customer reviews and that offers a platform for the audience to connect with your brand.

Search Engine Marketing (SEO & PPC)

In Asia, local search engines are more dominant when compared to 'international' ones such as Google. As such, marketers looking to optimize for Asia must take into consideration the requirement for localizing a website in each individual country that they target. It is also recommendable to take a two-pronged approach that entails including both international and local search engines in your SEO strategy for Asia. For example, a site targeting the Chinese market cannot simply use Google or Yahoo and overlook the local search engine Baidu that is more popular than Google in the country.

When optimizing for the Asian audience, language localization is essential. This does not just entail direct translation of copy, lists and keywords. Effective localization entails establishing a website that takes into consideration the nuances of the local culture. Therefore, your SEO campaign should take into account the individual and unique features of each market and the way in which the local audiences discuss products, services and brands. As such, it is important for marketers to undertake research and test the language translations in the context of each target country to better reach out to the target audience in these countries.

While Google plays a significant role in Asia as in other parts of the world (Asia accounts for 38% of the total Google global searches), local search engines dominate search in the Asian market. The dominant player in China is Baidu, which carters to the majority of web users who search in Chinese. Baidu accounts for an estimated 60% share of the search market in the county and is in fact more popular than the primarily English search engine, Google. Baidu has also partnered with Bing and as such, continues to predominate search in China. This search engine is significantly similar to Google and is set up on both organic search and pay-per-click search. In addition, the ad placement is similar to Google's with the ads charged on a pay-per-click basis and placed at the top right side of the interface, while the organic ads are placed at the center. Baidu is configured for the Chinese language and it thus performs better than Google in this regard. Baidu and Google account for more than 40% of paid search advertising spend each in Asia Pacific.

In Japan, Google currently powers the organic search for Yahoo Japan, while Yahoo Japan continues to provide paid search on a pay-per-click basis. In addition to Yahoo Japan as a search engine, web users also utilize it as an actual website and it remains one of the most visited sites in the country. The search behavior of Japanese contributes to portals generating greater traffic than the sole search engines. Japan ranks third in the world in volume of searches conducted by its users.

In South Korea, Naver is the dominant search engine accounting for up to 65% of the country's search market. Other international search engines including Yahoo and Google account for just 7% of the market in South Korea, combined. In spite of Google's efforts to localize its platform to act more as a portal, Naver has been able to dominate because it is configured to overcome the language and translation challenges. Naver also boasts a high penetration for online shopping, making it a more trusted portal than global search engines. Paid searches are more dominant on Naver than organic search ads, which only occupy a small section at the bottom of the page. Businesses can list their paid search more than once on the same page.

In India, Google is undoubtedly the leading search engine taking up 90% of the market. Yahoo follows Google with up to 8% of the search market and Bing comes third with 2%. In India 40% of the total Google searches are conducted on mobile devices.

In conclusion, when optimizing for Asia, site translation is just one element. Moreover, while funneling traffic to the site using search engine marketing it is equally important to understand the workings of local search engines for effective lead generation and relevant traffic.

In Asia, the concept of search engine marketing is fairly new. However, marketers are increasingly leveraging the growing trends of mobile use among Asian web users. Asians search frequently using their mobile phones, as much as they use these mobile devices to check their email. Businesses looking to market and promote their online enterprises using SEM techniques must configure their websites for mobile access.

As in other parts of the world, search is used variously in Asia. In China, web users utilize search engines to aggregate information and for price comparison. A large majority of the web users are inclined to make online purchases from the sites they have searched. Most people will buy electronics including phones and computers online after they have searched the company.

In India, web users utilize search for price comparison and to analyze product features. In addition, like in China, a large majority of these consumers will purchase online from sites they have searched.

Korea has a large population that undertakes search and is willing to purchase online. However, unlike India and China where consumers are more likely to purchase electronics than any other product online, Koreans are willing to purchase products and services across a wide range. These include entertainment, education, health and beauty, electronics and games.

According to the digital marketing agency, iProspect, it is advisable that marketers optimize their website content within the search funnels to ensure that consumers are targeted at each level of the sales process. Asians are very keen on price as much as they are on value. Thus, search plays a significant role in their purchase decision.

It is also advisable to optimize for more than one search engine in your search campaigns in each target market. As illustrated previously, local search engines are more dominant in Asia but global players are also present and play an important role in the search dynamics of the Asian market. Additionally, marketers will find that the pay-per - click inventory as well as organic search performance is different for each search engine in individual markets. By using several search engines, marketers will be better placed to fully engage with their target audience in each country.

According to a survey by MasterCard on online shopping trends, up to 80% of participants in China and Thailand engage in online shopping. This makes these two countries the most dominant online shoppers in the Asia-Pacific region. Japan comes in third with an estimated 75% while Korean web users come in fourth with up to 72% of the online shopping market share.

The study further shows that up to 60% of web users in the Asia-Pacific region largely depend on social media networks to make purchasing decisions, compared to just 43% of global web users. Online customer review and recommendations play an important role in determining whether one will purchase a product or service. The online shoppers and web users in Asia are also more likely to air their opinion on social networking sites about a product, service or brand that they had a negative experience with.

Social Media Marketing

Web users in Asia are among the most active, when compared to global averages and trends. According to Global Web Index, a large percentage of Asian web consumers are engaged in instant messaging, photo sharing and uploading, blogging and micro-blogging as well as webmail usage. Other studies by We Are Social indicate that some Asian countries are actively engaged in social media, while others are largely lagging behind. Brunei, Hong Kong and South Korea have a social media penetration of up to 50% when compared to the regional averages that loom at about 20%.

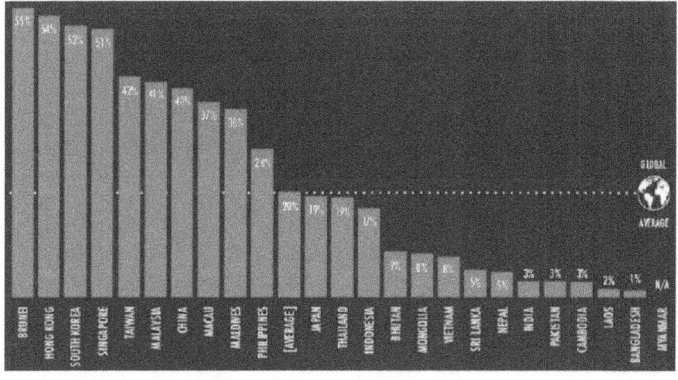

The social network Qzone is the top social network in China and is more popular than Facebook, accounting for about 536 million users. Other popular social networking sites in China include Tencent Weibo (310 million users) and the micro-blogs Sina Weibo (250 million users). Web users prefer Renren to Facebook in China and use Youku Tuduo for video streaming (up to 310 million video viewership each day) more than they use YouTube. The average Chinese social media user has 2.78 social profiles (We Are Social).

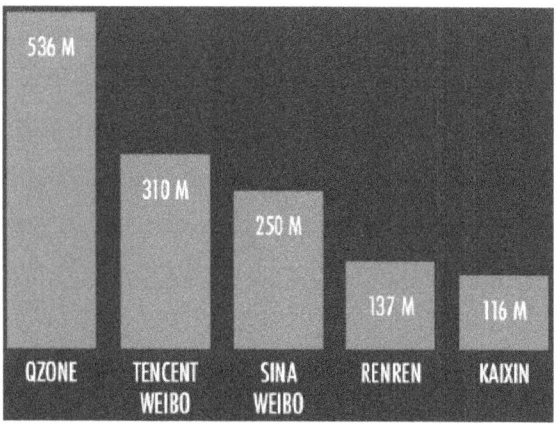

Cyworld in South Korea, Mixi in Japan, Wretch in Taiwan and Zing in Vietnam are also well known social networks in Asia.

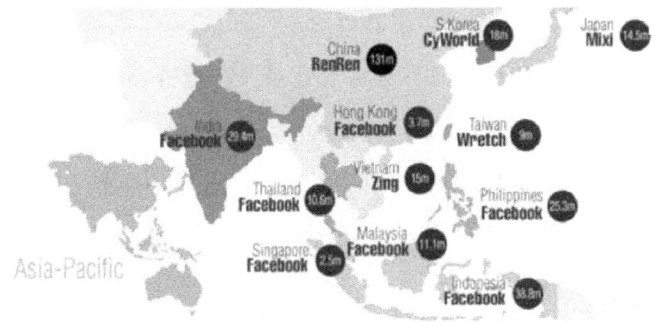

In Vietnam according to We Are Social, Zing, Facebook and Yume are the most popular social networks.

In South Korea, Cyworld is the most popular social networking platform attracting up to 25 million users (We Are Social).

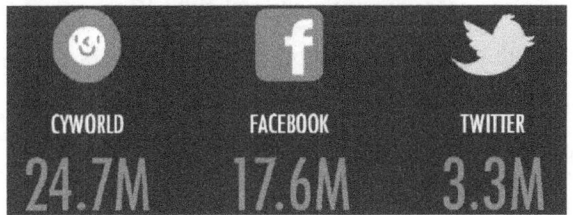

South Korea presents a particularly lucrative market for global business and online marketers. The population is largely tech savvy and the country has one of the highest Internet penetrations with up to 67% of the population having access to speedy Internet connection. Me2Day is equally a popular micro-blogging site catering to the active blogging and micro-blogging community in South Korea.

However, Facebook is still a popular social network in some Asian countries (25% market share) most notably in the Philippines (the biggest Facebook penetration in the world with 94% reach), India (the third largest Facebook market after the U.S. and Brazil with 50 million users), Indonesia (the fourth largest Facebook market with 40 million users), Thailand, Singapore and Malaysia. All these countries account for up to 172 million Facebook users combined.

India, in spite of its mammoth population, has only a social media penetration rate of 3%, which is one of the lowest rates in the Asia-Pacific region. Most of the social media users in India are predominantly engaged with Facebook (31 million) than they are with any other social network. The predominance of Facebook in India is attributable to the fact that Facebook has localized its services to include the diverse language dialects in the country. In India, Facebook is available in Telugu, Malayalam, Bengalis, Punjabi and Hindi. India has the second highest number of users in the world in Linkedin, Google+ and YouTube.

In Japan, Mixi has the largest following as a social networking site with over 17 million users (We Are Social).

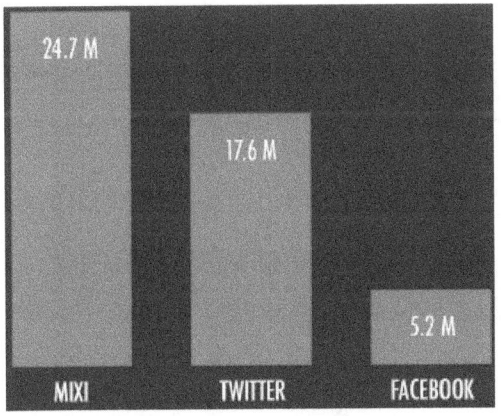

A large majority of social media users (up to three quarters) in the country access social networking platforms from their mobile phones. Japan has some of the continent's highest 3G penetration, accounting for 95%. In Japan, local social media sites are more popular than global ones, which generally cater to an English speaking audience. After the U.S. and India, Japan accounts for the largest number of YouTube users with up to 8% of the market share. The popularity of gaming in the Japan accounts for the large engagement with YouTube that users demonstrate. Web users generally utilize Facebook and Twitter for content sharing. Japanese is the second most popular language on Twitter and the country produces 25% of the global tweets while Indonesia accounts for 15% of the global tweets. The largest social gaming platform in Japan, Mobage has 30 million registered users.

Singapore also presents a lucrative market for social media marketing. The country boasts some of the highest high-speed Internet penetration in the region at 167%, according to internetworldstats.com. There are more than 4 million users in the country who have access to Internet both at home and at work. This is about 78% of the country's population. Singaporeans spend more than 7 hours weekly on social networking sites (We Are Social).

While social media marketing is a growing trend in Asia, businesses have not yet fully utilized the opportunity that Social Media Marketing presents. It is not uncommon to find that most of the social media accounts set up by businesses are inactive or infrequently updated. For a large majority of businesses social media marketing is more of a short-term strategy than it is a long-term one. This is quite a contrast to trends in the Western countries where more and more businesses are leveraging the full potential of social media networks.

In Asia, China and South Korea are seen as the continent's social media leaders in the corporate segment. This can be attributed to the blogging culture that has caught up in these two countries. Taiwan and Singapore generally have a conservative business culture, thus they demonstrate some of the lowest social media penetration in the region. Japanese users are posting more than one million blogs a month, more than any country in the region. More than 220 million people in China have blogs.

Email Marketing

In the Western Europe and in the U.S., marketers utilize email marketing as a cost effective strategy for customer engagement and relationship building. Email marketing in these regions can also be an effective method of sales generation. Gmail accounts for 39% of webmail traffic. Email is the preferred method for Indians and Japanese online consumers to receive information from marketers.

However, email marketing in Asia is admittedly not as developed as it is in the West; in China 80% of the emails go missing. The reason for this has been the logistical challenges of catering to a diverse market. In Asia, brands find it increasingly costly to translate content into different languages; they are faced with exorbitant costs in content creation, insufficient data and stringent government oversight. On the consumer end, email is not a popular form of communication; instant messaging is preferable in Asia.

Language barriers are one of the main reasons why marketers have not been fully successful in utilizing the potential of email marketing in Asia. Marketing campaigns tend to be designed in regional offices and the campaign would have to be rolled out in over 10 countries. Asia is highly fragmented in terms of culture and languages and implementing an email marketing campaign across these different segments can be challenging. In addition to the daunting task of translating copy into multiple languages, marketers are faced with the task of optimizing for the different market segments in the continent.

The language differences in Asia have made the use of mobile phones and instant messaging more popular than email; people can communicate with their social network and families in their own language. As such, marketers are increasingly integrating their email marketing campaigns with instant messages to reach out to the audience in Asia.

Another obstacle facing marketers is the problem of spam, which is prevalent in Asia. As such, many consumers in the continent have become apprehensive about providing their information to avoid being flooded with spam emails. Marketers and businesses looking to launch email-marketing campaigns in this market have to put in more effort to persuade consumers that they will only receive relevant content and not spam emails.

Social media platforms can be a great source of quality consumer data including email addresses. One way to do this is to embed useful or interesting content such as funny image or video clips in social media platforms and accompany this with an opt-in. After gaining the attention of your target audience, follow this up with incentives such as coupons and gifts. You will be surprised at how willing the market here will be to offer their information.

An interesting trend is the integration of email marketing with mobile usage in Asia. Tech savvy countries such as China, Japan, South Korea, Hong Kong and Singapore are consistently developing new ways of using mobile devices.

Mobile is fast becoming the preferred method of accessing email among web users in the region. As such, marketers looking to engage with the Asian audience should optimize their email campaign for mobile accessibility. It is also essential to optimize for different platforms including iPhones and Android mobile devices.

Mobile Marketing

Mobile marketing involves the use of mobile devices to engage with your target audience. With mobile marketing, consumers may simply subscribe to receive messages concerning a brand and its product. The popularity of mobile marketing can be attributed to the fact that it is a low cost method of traffic and sales generation. This form of marketing is also less intrusive and consumers may be more willing to engage with a brand through mobile devices than emails, more so in Asia. The most used mobile device in South East Asia is the iPad according to marketingmag.com.au.

Top 10 most used mobile devices in South East Asia

1. Apple iPad   32.0%
2. Apple iPhone   19.1%
3. RIM BlackBerry Curve 8520   3.5%
4. RIM BlackBerry Onyx (aka Bold) 9700   2.2%
5. Apple iPod touch   1.9%
6. Nokia C3-00   1.6% $179
7. Samsung Galaxy Tab P1000   1.4%
8. Nokia 5130 XpressMusic   1.2%
9. Samsung Galaxy Mini S5570   1.2%
10. RIM BlackBerry Curve 9300 3G   1.2%

Android is the leading operating system in both China and Japan. 66% of the smartphone owners in China access social networks on their mobile device daily and 59% of the Chinese smartphone owners have purchased via their device compared to 39% in Japan (Our Mobile Planet). China has more than 252 million smartphone users.

Operating System

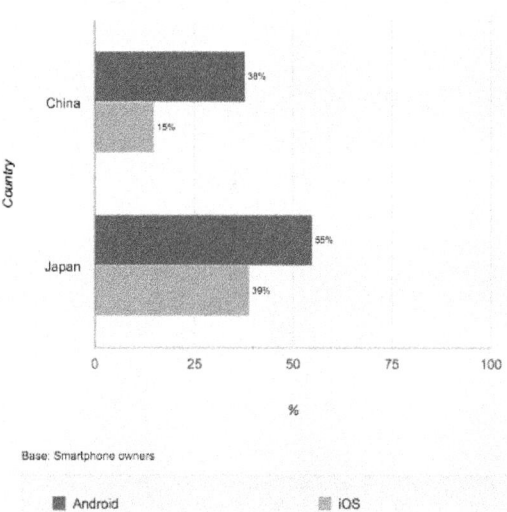

Base: Smartphone owners

■ Android   ■ iOS

Frequency of social network visits on smartphone

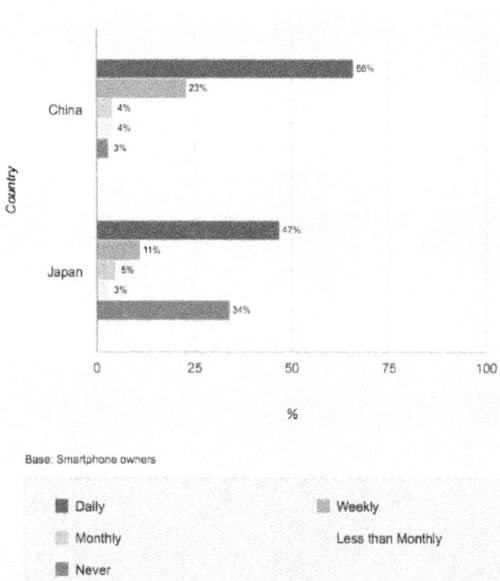

Base: Smartphone owners

■ Daily   ■ Weekly
■ Monthly   Less than Monthly
■ Never

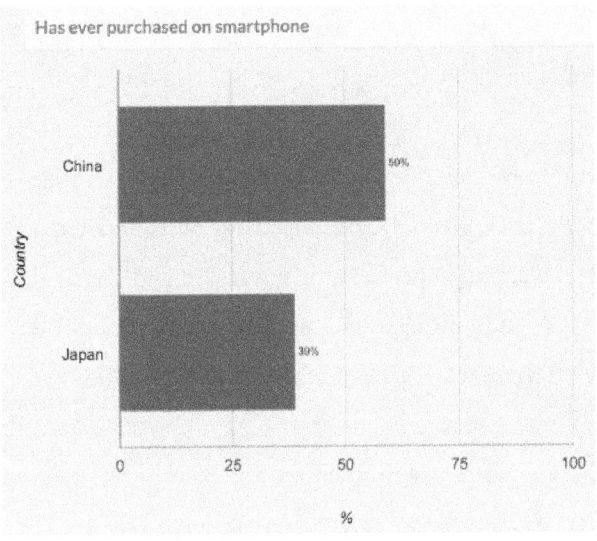

Has ever purchased on smartphone

67% of the ecommerce in India comes from mobile devices. In terms of mobile subscribes both India and China have similar numbers, which is approx. 900 million. Singapore and Hong Kong lead Asia for mobile penetration with more than 1.5 devices per user. Filipinos lead the world in SMS usage with 2 billion SMS sent every day (700 SMS per user).

After the U.S., Asia has the largest number of mobile phone usage. Japan has the largest number of iPhone users in the continent and comes in fourth globally. Similarly, Japan boasts highly developed data and network services. The country also has an advanced audience in terms of online engagement in mobile social networking, mobile browsing as well as online video chatting.

Singapore too has one of the region's highest iPhone penetration rates, given the fact that most of its population is urban. The country accounts for the region and the world's highest IOS (iPhone operating system) penetration; one in every ten Singaporeans accesses the web using an iOS.

In the Philippines and Indonesia, the Blackberry is more popular than the iPhone. Most users in these countries use their smartphones for instant messaging and engagement with the Twitter platform.

Malaysia and Thailand, besides Singapore, represent the largest iPhone market share in the region. However, just a small niche market of up to 0.5% accounts for the countries' iPhone users.

According to a recent study by Google Mobile Ads, smartphone owners in the region use their smartphones in conjunction with other media including TV, surfing the Internet and listening to music. The study shows that more than 53% of smartphone owners in Japan use their mobile devices when they are surfing or watching TV-the smartphone is an integral part of their day-to-day engagement with media even when they are consuming other forms of media.

Up to 87% of Chinese interviewed in the (above-mentioned) study report to have carried out a mobile search after they saw an offline ad. This trend is also prevalent in other markets including Japan with up to 62% smartphone users utilizing their mobile devices to search for an ad they saw on TV.

In addition to using their smartphones to search for ads, users in the region also use their mobile devices to find local businesses. This trend is especially popular in China and Japan where up to 95% and 97% of interviewed participants report that they use their phones to look for local service/product providers.

Smartphone users in the region also frequently use their phones for online purchases. In China up to 78% of smartphone users make a mobile purchase once each month. In the same vein, up to 51% of users in Japan make a purchase through their phones at least once each month.

In the greater part of Asia and South East Asia in particular, most owners of mobile phones use prepaid services. Users are very keen on price and most of them shop for bargains for the best deals. In countries such as the Philippines, it is very common for users to have more than two SIM cards in an attempt to take advantage of any bargain offers from the available service providers. While this may be beneficial for mobile phone users, it is difficult for service provides to establish brand loyalty or profit from premium services.

Affiliate Marketing

Asians have engaged in affiliate marketing for a long time. However, unlike in Europe or North America where most businesses use third party networks to manage their affiliate programs, in Asia most businesses establish their networks and manage them independently.

One reason for this is that launching an affiliate program in the region can be challenging due to the language barriers. Ecommerce is also not fully developed in the region, but this is slowly changing as more and more people choose to shop online. Consumers in Asia are more inclined to shop for services online including rental space services, travel and hotel reservation, payment of bills and concert tickets.

Other challenges that face affiliate marketing in Asia are the creation and publication of multilingual content for websites. Creating a site with several languages will require you to establish affiliate managers to oversee affiliates in all these languages. There is also the obstacle of multiple currency payment, the varying ecommerce regulations in each country and issues of national censorship.

Today local and in-county affiliate networks are inevitably more popular in Asia than 'global' affiliate networks such as ClickBank, Amazon Affiliate, Commission Junction or Affiliate Windows. The affiliate marketing landscape in Japan is one of the most developed in the region with local popular affiliate networking platforms such as Pocket Affiliate, Smart C, Traffic Gate, Access Trade, and Moba8 among others.

In Japan, affiliate marketing has indeed become an integral part of businesses in the country. However, unlike in the West where affiliate marketing can sometimes be frowned upon due to issues of fraud, this business practice is widely accepted in Japan. In fact, online marketers as well as big brands are actively engaged in affiliate marketing for lead generation as well as sales campaigns.

Other <u>regional affiliate marketing networks</u> include:

Zanox (Japanese)

ValueCommerce (Japanese)

U2Mee.com (Chinese)

LuckyPacific.com

LinkShare (Japanese)

JANet (Japanese)

clixGalore (Japanese)

ClickValue.cn (Chinese)

Chinese AN (China, Hong Kong, Taiwan)

Baidu Union (Chinese)

AsiaClickz

Allyes.com (Chinese)

Alimama (Chinese)

AdForBest.com

AccessTrade.net (Japanese)

8Affiliate.com

Video Marketing

Video marketing entails the use of online video platforms such as YouTube to promote a product to a targeted audience. In Asia, video marketing is increasingly an important element of business marketing campaigns. This is precipitated by the growing mobile and Internet connection penetration in the region as a whole.

According to the Nielsen Global Multi Screen Survey, carried out between August 31 and September 16, 2011, the video marketing trends in the Asia-Pacific region account for approximately $1.5 billion. The survey also projects an annual growth of 19% in the coming four years.

Yet in spite of the fact that companies are beginning to embrace and invest in video marketing, only 33% of the target market trusts video advertisements. Additionally only 36% of those interviewed report that the marketing message on the videos was relevant to the type of information they were looking for concerning a product.

The study also showed that up to 80% of the web users in Asia watched an online video, compared to the global average of 74%. Up to 68% view online videos at least once each week. The Philippines has the highest rate of online video viewership with up to 84% of the online users consuming video content once each week.

Online platforms such as YouTube not only act as hosts for promotional video ads, consumers are increasingly using these platforms as social media networks where they go to, to read reviews about a product before making the decision to purchase. The study by Nielsen Global shows that up to

81% of consumers in Vietnam are likely to turn to platforms such as YouTube to view an ad and to check out reviews before making a decision to purchase. The trend is also high in China and Thailand where 77% and 69% of consumers rely on online video ads and reviews to guide their purchasing decisions. The average Japanese online user watches 160 videos per month and 70% of the Indian Internet users watches online videos (We Are Social).

Digital advertising attracts a higher return on investment globally and in fact accounts for up to 16% of advertising expenses globally. However, the amount allocated to online video advertisement in the Asia Pacific region is not as prominent as one would expect. Marketers are yet to tap into the potentially lucrative opportunity offered by online video marketing, to reach the target audience.

Ecommerce

An online shopping survey by the Nielsen Company shows that consumers in Asia are among the most prolific online shoppers. More than a third (up to 35%) of those engaged in the survey report that they spend up to 11% of their shopping budget online. The global averages for online shoppers are about 27%. 80% of the online Asian population claims to have made an online purchase (NielsenWire).

Among the consumers in the Asia-Pacific region, retail sites with an online presence only, are more popular. Additionally, up to 30% of those interviewed in the survey report to frequenting retail sites that allowed them to choose products from various stores.

Ecommerce is largely immature in China when compared to countries such as Japan, Taiwan, Singapore and Thailand. Online shoppers in China (approx. 200 million spending an average of 5 hours weekly shopping online) mostly purchase footwear, apparels, music, films and books. Each minute 48,000 new items are sold on taobao.com.

Overall, ecommerce in Asia still lacks penetration when one takes into consideration the volume of Internet users in the region. However, the rate at which Asians are adopting online selling and buying is more impressive when compared to similar markets in Western Europe and North America.

eMarketer predicts that in the next years leading up to 2015, China will lead in the ecommerce global growth with an estimated 95%, compared to the expected global ecommerce growth of 12% in North America.

Even though ecommerce penetration in Asia is still lower when compared to penetration in Europe and North America, this low penetration is compensated for by several volume metrics. For example, emerging markets such as Indonesia, China and India have immense populations and up to 50% of global Internet users, are found in these emerging economies. Moreover, the average expenditure for every active Internet shopper in the region is about $610, according to eMarketer.

One of the challenges that brands and online retailers may face with ecommerce in Asia is the diverse chasm between developed markets and those that are just emerging. E-retailers and brands would have to highly segment their ecommerce efforts when launching in Asia. The returns and level of engagement from consumers will vary greatly from one economy to the other. However, mobile penetration in the region continues to make it easier for consumers to make online purchases locally and globally too.

Local ecommerce sites seem to be more popular in Asia than 'global' ecommerce sites. Some of these popular online retail sites include:

T-mall: Alibaba owns T-mall. It is a market leader, particularly in China where it accounts for about 40% of the market share. The site sells just about anything from apparels, to books and luxury cars. The site also offers an ecommerce platform for some of its competitors and hosts big brands such as Pepsi.

360Buy.com: This site accounts for up to 15% of the market share in China. The site primarily serves as an online storefront for electronics, books, home appliances as well as apparels. It also hosts an online travel service and a luxury mall for high-end brands at 360Top.com.

Rakuten: Popular ecommerce sites in Japan are Yahoo! Japan and Rakuten. Rakuten has up to 47 million users and the company has hired an international workforce. While it does not stock its own products, it offers an online platform for smaller e-retailers to trade their products.

Gmarket: In Korea, Gmarket is the largest and most popular ecommerce site. The site also caters to a global audience looking for Korean products and as such offers worldwide shipping.

Flipkart and eBay: are some of the largest and most popular e-retail sites in India. Flipkart is estimated to be valued at $1billion. Unlike Flipkart, which only offers a platform for people to buy products, eBay allows people to advertise their products and others to sell on the same site.

Methods Of Payment

In Asia, credit cards are not as widely used as they are in Western Europe or North America. One of the main reasons why Alibaba is successful and among the most popular ecommerce platforms in the region is because it allows customers to do direct bank transfers from their debit accounts.

Almost all ecommerce platforms in China, India, Hong Kong and Taiwan allow customers to pay through escrow accounts in addition to accepting regular debits cards, credit cards and bank transfers. Tenpay and Alipay are the main providers of escrow payment services in China. BillDesk and CCAvenue are the main providers in India while AsiaPay mainly carters to the market in Hong Kong.

In China, the shipping costs are considerably low and this offers ecommerce an advantage in the country. However, customers with larger orders tend to spend more on tracking services. In the territory of Taiwan, delivery service providers have partnered with local convenience stores to distribute orders to these stores, which are close to the customer's workplace or residence. This largely reduces the cost of shipment and delivery.

In most countries there is no special tax for online purchases but the customs authority in each country have their own regulations. Generally, custom is paid for goods that are valued over a certain threshold. Goods that are marked as gifts may not attract boarder tax, even though the good is in fact bought.

Alibaba is one of the largest and among the most popular sites for online shopping in Asia. This can be attributed to the fact that Asians generally prefer local portals and are more loyal to these platforms than they are to global ones. Additionally, as seen above, trust plays a significant role in Asian business. Alibaba is an established site and thus attracts more shoppers who feel they can trust the site enough to make purchases.

A significant factor that has popularized Alibaba is its conducive payment methods. Alipay allows customers to make direct transfers from their banks and has partnered with leading banks in China. Other than eBay, Alibaba seems to be the preferred option for online shoppers in the region to purchase goods abroad.

7
Online Marketing In Latin America

Latin America is an emerging market that offers promising opportunities for global business. While Brazil (80 million Internet users), Mexico (42 million Internet users) and Argentina (28 million Internet users) are large economies that offer huge potential, other countries such as Columbia, Chile, Peru, and Uruguay also present growing opportunities for businesses seeking to expand to Latin America. The online population in the region is one of the fastest growing in the world. There are approx. 40% of the Latino Americans online that is 240 million Internet users, same number as in the U.S. and half of the Internet users in Europe. Latin America accounts for 10% of the global Internet audience with Brazil having the 5th largest Internet population (40% Internet penetration) after China, the U.S., India, and Japan. More than 32.5% of the Latin America online users are aged 15-24 (comSocre).

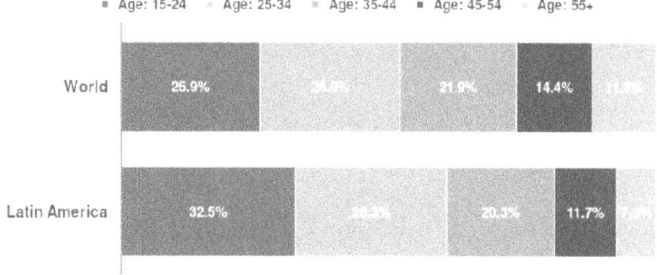

The online growth in the Latin America can be attributed to the ever-growing broadband penetration and increasing online sophistication. Thus, if you have not yet considered expanding to Latin America, here is why you should:

Cultural Differences: Dos And Don'ts

When marketing to the Latin America audience it is important that you take into consideration the cultural and business nuances of your audience. Latin America is a diverse region and even though most countries may share language and some cultural attributes, it is imperative to approach each country as a unique market. Instant messaging usage in Latin America leads the world with 70% reach compared to the worldwide average of 39.3%.

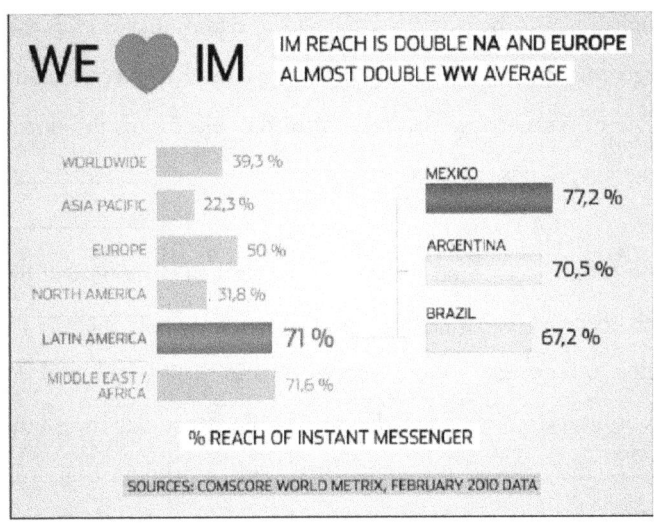

WE ♥ IM   IM REACH IS DOUBLE **NA** AND **EUROPE** ALMOST DOUBLE **WW** AVERAGE

WORLDWIDE	39,3 %
ASIA PACIFIC	22,3 %
EUROPE	50 %
NORTH AMERICA	31,8 %
LATIN AMERICA	71 %
MIDDLE EAST / AFRICA	71,6 %

MEXICO 77,2 %
ARGENTINA 70,5 %
BRAZIL 67,2 %

% REACH OF INSTANT MESSENGER

SOURCES: COMSCORE WORLD METRIX, FEBRUARY 2010 DATA

When doing business in Latin America, you should practice patience. Business and decision-making processes take time in Latin America and it may seem as if your audience is taking too long to come to a decision. Business in the region primarily hinges on personal relationships and you may wait longer to win over your audience.

As mentioned earlier, it is important for businesses to approach each territory uniquely because what may sell in Argentina may not necessarily appeal to the market in Mexico. It will also be seen as cultural insensitivity to approach one country the same way you would another.

English is not the primary language of communication in the large majority of countries in Latin America. You might have to familiarize yourself with the basics of the local language, to pass a message across.

You really need to ensure that your product offering will be well received by your target audience. Generally, people in Latin America like to look successful and this is expressed by the physical things they have. While most will not buy exorbitantly priced products, they want a product that will uplift their status. As such, it is beneficial to research and find out the products that your target audience values for their status.

Unlike trends in Western Europe, Australia or U.S., where people want to get straight to business, Latin Americans are looking to build a relationship first. Before getting into the details of price and products, be sure to establish a relationship with your audience first. If your audience feels connected to you, they are more likely to engage with your business.

Latin Americans are generally committed to the group, more so the family. It is important that you respect these group bonds, even though you might be more inclined to individualism. From a marketing point of view, you will be essentially selling to a collectivity rather than an individual as consumers tend to make decisions according to input from their family and social networks.

The Latin American society is primarily risk averse and does not easily accept change or something that is unfamiliar. As such, new global businesses seeking to penetrate the market will have to go an extra mile to persuade their target audience about their brand and product offering.

Website Design And Customer Engagement

There are up to 240 million Internet users in Latin America and this presents a large audience for a Latin American website. As you design a website for this audience, one of the challenges you may face is localizing the website in Spanish. While Spanish is generally widely used in most countries in the region, the versions and variations are different.

To truly adapt your site to all your target countries, it is beneficial to understand the language nuances in each country. This will involve extensive research as well as assistance from a native translator who understands the Spanish language variations in each of these countries.

People in Latin America are typically colorful and celebrative. Consider this when designing the website; include bright colors such as yellows, oranges, greens and pinks as these symbolize festivity that is at the heart of Latin American culture. In addition, due to the artistic nature of Latin American culture, your audience is likely to appreciate graphics that represents the unusual and come out as energetic and soulful. Be liberal when using graphics for a Latin American audience and be sure to bring out the celebrative feel to the site.

Latin Americans are closely tied to their families, close friends, and typically reach out to this social network for recommendations before making a decision to purchase. Testimonials from their social networks are very important to them. Thus, when creating a website offer a platform for your audience to provide and read reviews about your brand and product offering.

Your audience in Latin America is also more willing to engage with a brand through social media, a blog or website. This is a contrast from an audience in New Zealand where people are less willing to engage with a brand unless for a special offer. Be sure to offer a platform through your website or blog that will allow your audience to engage with you directly.

Search Engine Marketing (SEO & PPC)

Consumers in the region are avid and curious searchers. According to a recent study by comScore on the search engine market in Latin America, 9 out of 10 searches carried out in Latin America were done on a Google-owned website. In 2011 search queries in the region increased by 21% accounting for up to 9 billion queries in the single month that the study was conducted. The average searcher in the region conducts up to 170 queries every month. Colombia leads the world in the average number of searches per user with 233 searches.

Average Searches per Searcher

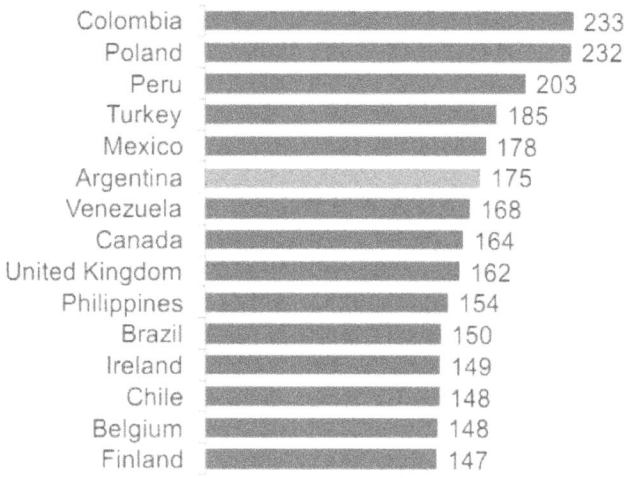

Colombia	233
Poland	232
Peru	203
Turkey	185
Mexico	178
Argentina	175
Venezuela	168
Canada	164
United Kingdom	162
Philippines	154
Brazil	150
Ireland	149
Chile	148
Belgium	148
Finland	147

The audience in Latin America also widely uses social media for search including Facebook, which accounts for 2.8% of the search market share and Microsoft Sites, which accounts for up to 2.8% of the share.

Consumers in the region search for various reasons including for information, social networking and commerce. The average searcher in Latin America spends up to 24 hours online each month and consumes approximately 1,795 pages of web content. The consumers in Brazil are generally the most prolific searchers with a large majority spending an average of 25.8 hours online.

One factor to consider when optimizing for Latin America is language localization. Decide whether you will use the global Spanish version for your content or the local variations of the language. This will depend on your specific target audience; a more sophisticated audience is likely to search in universal Spanish. Nevertheless, localization will allow you greater visibility at the search engines.

The <u>search engine market share in Latin America</u> is approximately:

Google: 72%

Yahoo: 17%

MSN: 2%

Search marketing in Latin America offers a promising opportunity for businesses seeking to make their sites more visible to the audience in this region. This can be attributed to the search behavior of Latin Americans. As indicated previously, a large majority of Internet users are increasingly searching for information with countries such as Brazil generating up to 6 billion queries in any given month. This is followed by Mexico, which conducts up to 3.2 billion queries each month while Columbia conducts as many as 2.9 million searches monthly.

The industries that are most actively engaged in search marketing include the retail sector, classifieds, travel, finance and automotive industries. Local newspapers are also leveraging the search trends of their audiences and have taken their search marketing efforts to major search platforms including MSN and Yahoo.

Cost per click prices in the region are fairly low compared to prices in the U.S. This could be attributed to the fact that search engine marketing, as a marketing technique itself is yet to gain traction in the Latin American business platform. If the conversion rates in Latin America are as significant as those in Europe and U.S., then search engine marketers are certainly enjoying a high return on investment.

Direct marketers and advertisement agencies are spending up to $10,000 each month on paid placements. The Tele sales sector spends an estimated $1,000 each month while the small businesses and resellers are spending an average of $200 and $10 each month respectively.

In addition to using mainstream search engines such as Google, Latin Americans are increasingly using social search. Marketers in the region are following the trend and seeking to leverage the social search behavior of the audience. Up to

20 million Internet consumers in the region have signed up with Yahoo Answers. This shows the level of engagement Latin Americans have when it comes to searching for information. Yahoo portals in the region have linked Yahoo Answers results to mainstream or standard search results.

Marketers who are looking to undertake search marketing in Latin America cannot overlook the importance of integrating their search marketing campaign with social search platforms.

Social Media Marketing

Latin America has a vast audience that is actively and consistently engaged in social media. While Facebook is largely dominated by users from the U.S., India and Germany, Latin America has one of the highest Facebook penetration rates. According to a comScore study *'The Rise of Social Networking in Latin America'*, the top five markets with the highest Facebook penetration rates are in Latin America.

In Chile, Facebook accounts for up to 91% of the social media users in the country. The country ranks third after Philippines and Turkey as the country with the highest Facebook penetration. Other countries in the region with high Facebook and social media penetration include Peru and Columbia with Facebook accounting for up to 89% of social media users. In Venezuela, Facebook accounts for an estimated 86.9% of social media users in the country.

In Brazil, 23% of online time is spent on social networking sites. According to comScore (2011) an estimated 115 million users in Latin America are engaged with social networking sites, accounting for 96% of the online population in the region. Taking into account data from the past year, the number of users engaged in social networking has increased by 16%; the time that social network users spent on these platforms increased by 88%. The comScore survey also found that:

The audience in Latin America is extensively participating in social networking. 5 of the top 10 markets accounting for the highest amount of time spent on social media are in Latin America. In 2011, users in Argentina accounted for the highest number of hours spent online at 10 hours per month. 40% of the online Latin American users play social games.

Latin American social media users demonstrate an equal percentage of both male and female audiences. However, the female population spent more time on social media platforms than males did. Additionally users aged between 15 and 24 are the most engaged social media market segment in the region.

Facebook is the most popular social networking site in Latin America with more than 115 million users. Windows Live Profile comes in second accounting for over 36 million users, while Orkut is ranked third attracting up to 35 million users. Orkut is widely popular is Brazil. Twitter is the fourth most popular social network with 27 million users in the entire region. Google+ is also gaining significant traction attracting more than 28 million users in the past year alone. Badoo, the social network for meeting new people is also very popular in this region of the globe.

Interestingly Pinterest is also increasingly popular in the region. In the whole of Latin America, Pinterest has gained an estimated 1.3 million users as of April 2012. In Brazil, Pinterest accounts for 28% of the regions social media users, while it accounts for 16% of users in Mexico, and 10% in Argentina. Puerto Ricans spend the most amount of time on Pinterest, with visitors spending up to 24 minutes each day. Argentineans also spend a significant amount on the site accounting for 15 minutes.

Even though the Latin American market is extensively engaged in social networking, marketers seeking to tap into this market must take a market-by-market approach. The trends are different in each country, thus the need to approach each market uniquely. With adequate research, social media marketing in Latin America can offer immense opportunities for marketers looking to launch cost effective campaigns. For example, comScore data indicates that Argentineans spend the most time on social media. In Brazil, Orkut was the most visited social network, while in Chile Facebook is the most dominant. In Mexico, a large majority of social network users utilize Facebook for video viewing accounting for 33% of the online population.

In addition to social networking, presentation sharing is widely popular in the region, with 7 of the top 10 global markets for Slideshare.net are in Latin America. Peruvians are the most prolific users of SlideShare accounting for up to 16% of the online population in the last year (2011).

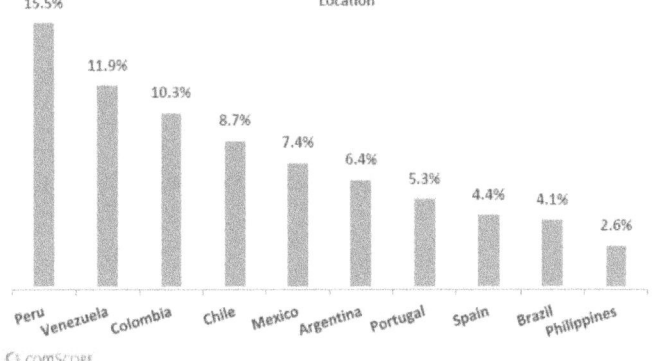

Top 10 Markets for Slideshare.net by % Reach of Visitors
Source: comScore Media Metrix, Jun-2011, Visitors Age 15+ Home/Work Location

The local social networking site Sonico is also a popular networking platform in Peru, accounting for up to 20% of the online market in the country. This makes Peru, the highest penetrated market for Sonico. In Venezuela, one out four users utilized Twitter in the last year (2011); this makes Venezuela among the most highly penetrated market for Twitter in the region.

5 of the top 10 Facebook global markets are in Latin America.

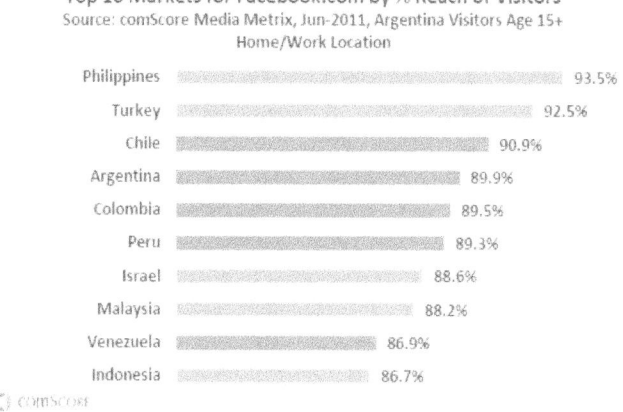

Top 10 Markets for Facebook.com by % Reach of Visitors
Source: comScore Media Metrix, Jun-2011, Argentina Visitors Age 15+
Home/Work Location

Philippines	93.5%
Turkey	92.5%
Chile	90.9%
Argentina	89.9%
Colombia	89.5%
Peru	89.3%
Israel	88.6%
Malaysia	88.2%
Venezuela	86.9%
Indonesia	86.7%

Globally, Brazil is the 3rd largest market for Google+, 2nd for Facebook and Twitter, and 4th for YouTube and Linkedin.

Overall, social media marketing in Latin America will continue to show steady growth given the popularity of social networking in the region. In contrast to the market in North America and other regions such as Asian and New Zealand, Latin Americans are more willing to engage with brands via social media. Marketers and businesses alike looking to expand into this region can leverage these trends. Currently only 39% of the Latin American companies have a

Facebook account (compared to 54% global average), 25% have YouTube accounts (compared to 50% global average) and 32% have Twitter accounts (compared to 65% global average). The Latin American companies post an average of 26 tweets per week and have an average of 2,626 followers (compared to 1,489 global average).

Companies with Facebook Accounts

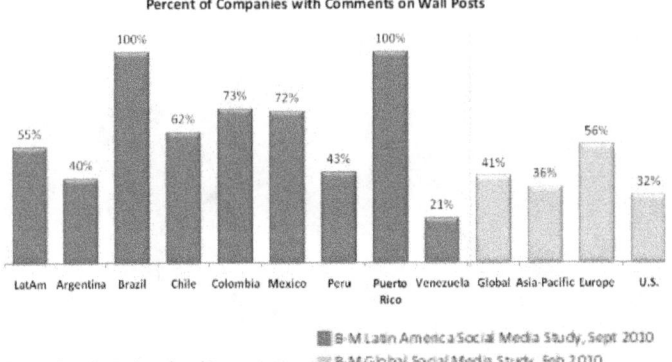

Percent of Companies with Comments on Wall Posts

B-M Latin America Social Media Study, Sept 2010
B-M Global Social Media Study, Feb 2010

Burson-Marsteller Evidence-Based Communications

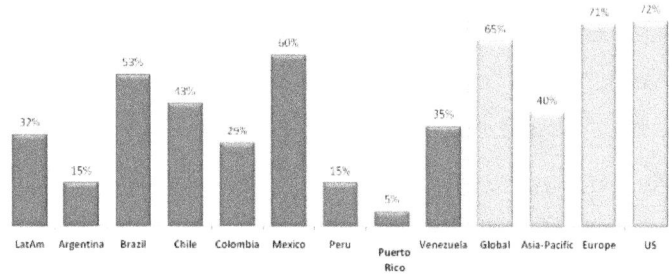

Companies with Twitter Accounts

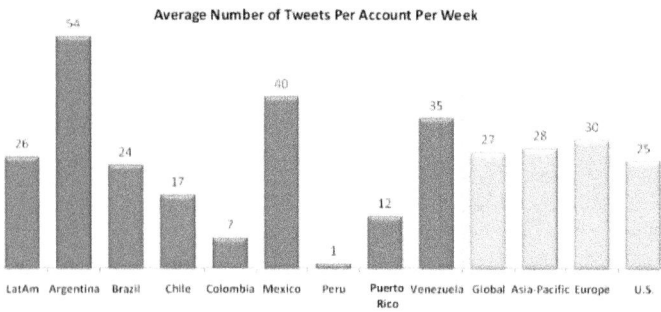

Average Number of Tweets Per Account Per Week

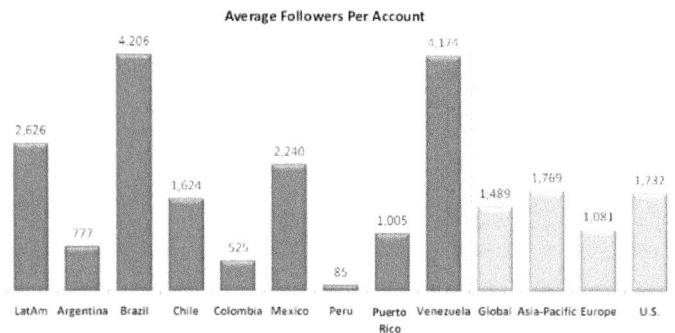

Average Followers Per Account

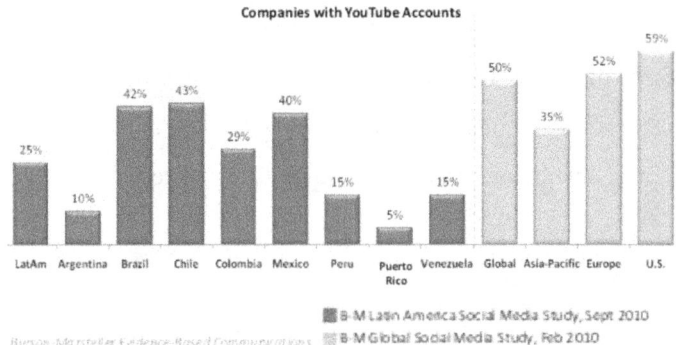

Companies with YouTube Accounts

■ B-M Latin America Social Media Study, Sept 2010		
▒ B-M Global Social Media Study, Feb 2010		

Burson-Marsteller Evidence-Based Communications

According to Forrester Research, up to 75% of urban online users in Brazil and Mexico for example are willing to connect with brands through social media. This is in contrast to users in the U.S. where only 47% expect a brand to have a social media presence. Additionally an average of 50% of the online market in the region view videos produced by a brand, as opposed to just 26% of online users in the U.S. The study shows that up to 30% of online users read a brand's blog and average of 15% of web users in the region follow a brand on Twitter, compared to just 4% of web users in the U.S.

Email Marketing

While social networking has gained traction in Latin America and Internet accessibility is wide spread, commercial email is still struggling to attain similar popularity. According to

Return Path, a leading email certification company, up to 30% of email from brands is viewed as spam and a large majority blocks marketing emails. Up to 10% of commercial opt-in emails are blocked by recipients in this region.

However, businesses in larger markets including Brazil and Mexico continue to use email for marketing to a much-targeted audience. Trust is a key issue with regard to email acceptance in this region. There are high incidences of online fraud and spamming, thus people are generally reluctant to give out information or to subscribe to a newsletter.

However, marketers can leverage the prolific social media usage in Latin to integrate email-marketing campaigns with social media. This integration can go a long way in generating warm leads to include in your email-marketing list. Integrating social with email will also allow you to get a better understanding of your audience before you begin to engage them with email marketing.

Mobile Marketing

Mobile Marketing entails the use of mobile to send promotional brand messages to a targeted audience that subscribes to receive these messages. The primary mode of mobile marketing entails SMS notifications, while other newer methods include the use of geo-location services, two dimension bar codes and GPS messaging.

Latin America has one of the highest rates of mobile device penetration in the world accounting for up to 56% according to eMarketer. Brazil has approx. 30% of the Latin America's mobile users. Smartphone penetration rate in Argentina, Mexico and Brazil stand at approximately 24%, 20%, and 14% respectively (Our Mobile Planet).

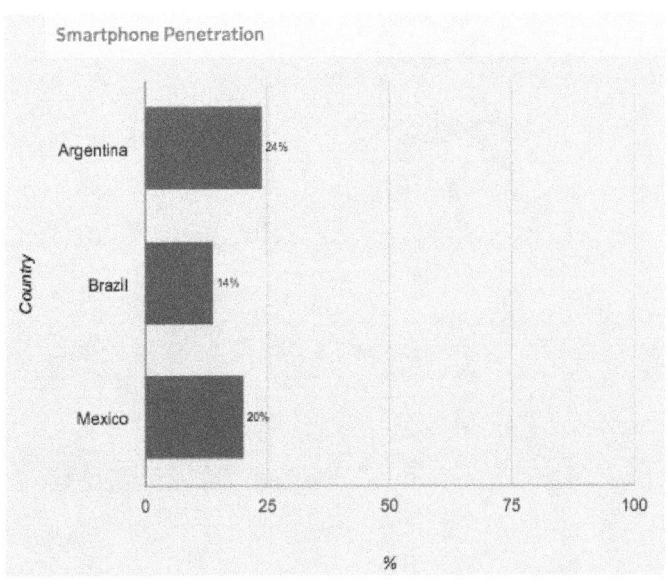

31% of the smartphone users in Brazil have purchased via their mobile device, 39% of the smartphone users in Argentina look daily for local information on their device and 73% of the Argentinian and Mexican smartphone users access social networks daily via their mobile device.

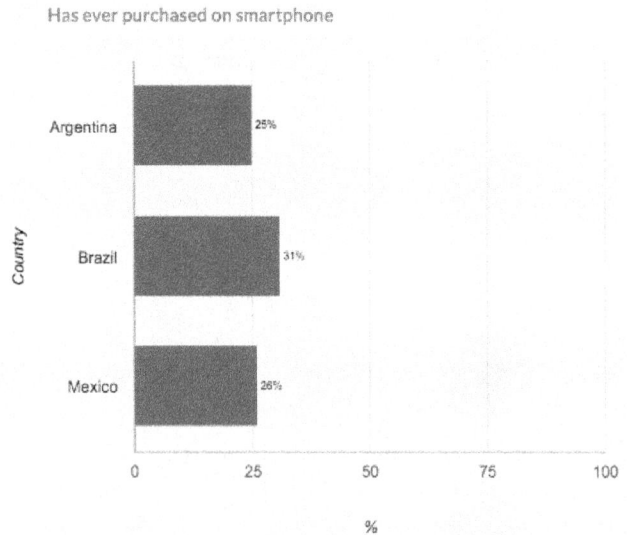

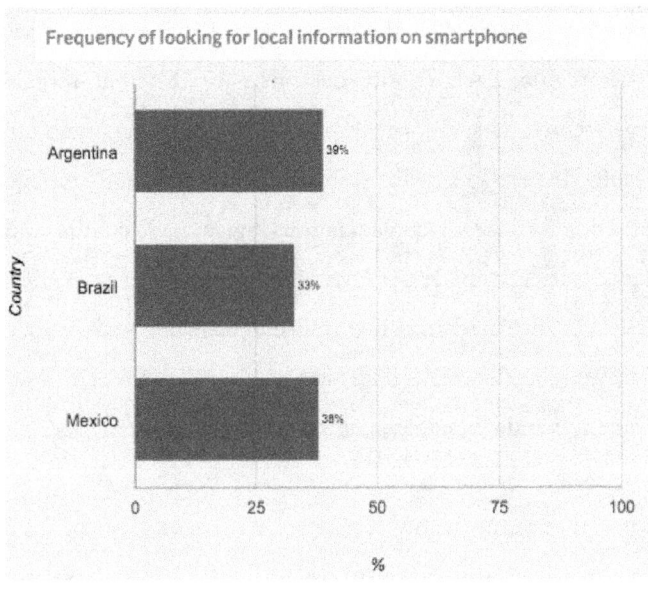

Frequency of looking for local information on smartphone

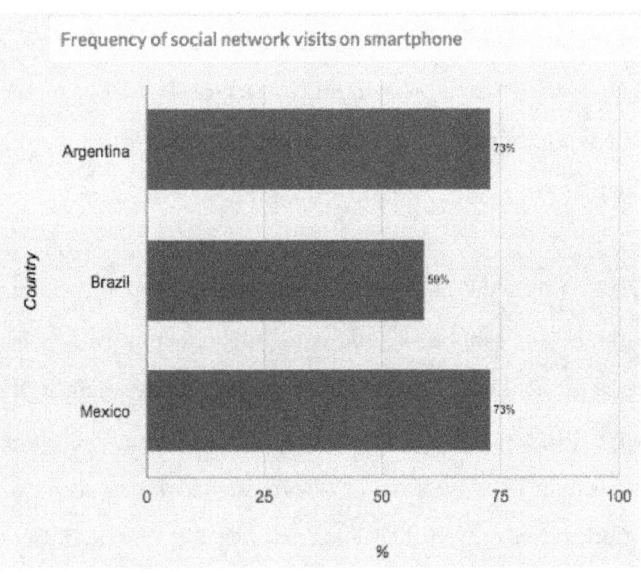

Frequency of social network visits on smartphone

However, regardless of the generally high penetration rates in the region, each county demonstrates different mobile usage trend. As such, it is important for marketers who are looking to engage with their audience through mobile marketing to take in considerations the unique culture and nuances of each market presented in Latin America. Other challenges that marketers might face in engaging with mobile marketing in the region include the limited prepaid user population and inadequate bandwidth.

Latin America has highly prized voice services as such, large number of consumers use prepaid mobile phones and extensively use SMS messages to communicate with family and friends. While data is expensive in the region, more and more carriers are now offering better deals to consumers such as unlimited data access, that can cost as much as one dollar a day.

Even as brands engage their audiences through mobile marketing, it can be beneficial to integrate this with social media given the high preference for social networking in the region. In Brazil and Mexico only, there is a mobile phone penetration of more than 76% offering marketers immense opportunity to reach their audience through mobile devices. However, to leverage this audience, it is essential to find the appropriate devices and applications suitable for this market. Just about 6% of mobile phone users utilize their phones to access Internet on a monthly basis and just 9% of the population in the region has a smartphone.

Mobile advertisement and marketing has been slow to pick up in Latin America, but there are promising indications that this trend will change with the growing number of smartphone ownership in the region.

According to comScore reports, mobile phones and tablet devices are increasingly attracting a significant amount of digital traffic. Puerto Rico demonstrates the highest digital traffic in terms of mobile device usage, accounting for up to 8% of all the digital traffic in the country.

According to comScore's Device Essentials report (2011) in Brazil, the highest amount of digital traffic is generated from mobile devices, primarily tablets, accounting for 40% of digital traffic generated in the country. Meanwhile tablets are equally popular in the region including Columbia where 39% of all digital traffic is in fact mobile web traffic. In Ecuador, the number is estimated at 32%, while in Mexico and Cost Rica mobile web traffic accounts for up to 28% in both countries.

Smartphone users in the region utilize their devices to find restaurants, jobs and vacation information. The increase in apps usage could be attributed to these mobile search trends. The Ipsos Media CT report shows that the consumers in Argentina installed an average of 16 applications on their smartphones of which four were paid for. In Brazil, users installed up to 14 applications and only two were paid for, while Mexican smartphone users installed an average of 18 applications, seven of which are paid applications. In addition to using their smartphones for search, consumers in this region also use their devices for video viewing, and accessing social networks.

Overall, Latin America has one of the fastest growing mobile phone penetration rates in the world. There are up to 630 million mobile phone users in the region, making Latin America the third largest mobile phone market after Asia and Africa. But the important factor here is not just that the region has a high mobile phone penetration rate; it is important that marketing professionals and brands understand the type of mobile phones that Latin Americans are buying and using. Smartphone penetration in the region is certainly poised to increase, offering early adopters an opportunity to connect with their target audience.

These developments have various implications for the region:

First, mobile is making Internet more accessible to consumers in Latin America. This means that Internet in the region will increase, providing greater opportunities for Internet marketing and global ecommerce. The online and mobile ad spend in Latin America is certainly bound to increase.

Given the reception that consumers are demonstrating, mobile advertising in Latin America has the potential to challenge search and display advertising.

Mobile Commerce
Admittedly, the use of mobile commerce is still in its infancy in Latin America, even in larger markets such as Brazil. However, there is an immense potential for mobile commerce in the region, in part due to an increase in the number of players coming in to the market. These players are developing advanced applications to facilitate different mobile transactions across all market segments.

Brazil shows considerable potential for m-commerce growth with ecommerce platforms such as Mercado making themselves more accessible through mobile phones. In addition, the social buying platform Clube de Desconto says that it has sold over 15,000 coupons through the iPhone application it developed to enable m-commerce.

Online games, dating sites and social network are also proving to be lucrative platforms for marketers looking to tap into m-commerce trends in the region. Due to the growing infrastructure for online payment, these platforms are now able to sufficiently monetize their services. Many businesses in the region are leveraging the Latin American culture of integrating mobile with social. The most convenient payment method for the online community in this region is increasingly becoming mobile, given the high penetration rates of mobile phones compared to the low penetration rates of easily accessible financial services.

Importantly, mobile ecommerce in Latin America is largely targeting those who are lower in the social economic ladder. Mainstream financial services are not widely accessible to this market segment, making mobile commerce a viable alternative.

Affiliate Marketing

While the online population in Latin America is on the fastest growing in the world, affiliate marketing is still a sector that is not widely established in the region. Unlike in nearby North America, affiliate marketing in Latin America has only just started picking up with local brands rolling out networks for sales generation. According to a Forrester Research, Latin America will experience the world's most significant growth in Internet advertising in the period between 2011 and 2012

While the growth of the online population in the region is remarkable, affiliate networking faces various challenges that have hindered its growth. First, there is a general inadequacy of affiliate solution providers in the region, forcing brands to establish and market their own affiliate programs. Businesses that are looking to establish region affiliate programs are likely to face other challenges including localization of the affiliate programs to suit each unique market as well adapting to language and currency differences in each country in the Latin American region.

Transparency is an important issue for Latin American affiliate marketing, with the most successful affiliate marketing programs being those that demonstrate high level of trust in the compensation structure. Successful affiliate programs such as MercadoLibre (an auction site) have been able to really adapt their affiliate programs to the different countries in the region. They have taken into consideration payment modalities as well cultural and language differences in setting up affiliates in major markets including Brazil, Argentina, Mexico, Columbia and Chile.

Earlier in 2000, Commission Junction began paying its affiliates in 30 different countries. The focus here was Europe and Asia and not Latin America. Today Commission Junction only offers payments in Mexican peso. Global affiliate marketing programs such as ClickBank and Amazon Affiliates have been slow to establish in Latin America. Other foreign affiliate programs seeking to tap into the growing online population in Latin America include Be Free and PlugInGo. Naturally, these brands have set up their affiliate programs in major markets including Brazil, Mexico and Argentina. Others include iMediation, multiKredits, eSpiral, Yupi.com

While the affiliate marketing landscape in Latin America is not yet as vibrant as it may be in North America, still offers an opportunity for early adopters and savvy brands looking to leverage the unsaturated markets.

Some of the well-known <u>affiliate networks</u> in the region include:

Adverlatin

Batanga Network

Fox Networks

Harren Media

MediaCom (Brazil)

Video Marketing

Video viewing in Latin America is a particularly popular phenomenon, more so among the younger generation. In the major markets of Argentina, Brazil, Chile and Mexico, up to 80% of the online population aged between 15 and 24 years watch online video content from work or at home, according to comScore (2011) reports. Brazil, which is home to the largest online population in the region accounts for up to 36 million video content consumers. In just a single month, the total amount of video content viewed averaged 3.1 billion. Mexico has the highest number of video content consumers with up to 88% of its Internet population consuming almost 2 billion online video content. The figures are equally impressive in Argentina where up to 12 million web consumers view online videos monthly, while in Chile up to 6.2 million people watch online videos.

The recent growth in video viewing can be attributed to the growing Internet penetration in the market. This makes video marketing in Latin America an area that marketers can consider leveraging for brand visibility in the region. According to comScore's recent webinar *Futuro Digital Latinoamerica*, Google Sites is the most popular video platform site in Mexico accounting for up to 20 million viewers. This trend is primarily attributable to YouTube viewership, which accounts for an estimated 68% of all online video content in the country. Additionally, web users watch an estimated 5 hours of video content on YouTube in any given month. Vevo is the second most popular video property attracting an average of 13 million users, while Vicom Digital comes in third with 6.4 million users.

For marketers looking to venture into the region with video marketing, the economy of scale presented by Latin America could be a point of advantage. Video is rapidly becoming an integral part of Latin American's interaction with the Web and this trend is duplicated in many countries in the region.

One obstacle facing video marketing in the region is low broadband and Internet connectivity. Compared to the Internet speeds in Asia, Western Europe and North America, Internet speeds in Latin America are still low.

However, this is gradually changing in major emerging markets such as Brazil, Mexico, Chile, Columbia and Argentina.

Ecommerce

Being a region that hosts a majority of the emerging economies in the world, Latin America is already demonstrating great potential for global ecommerce and is expected to be worth $73 billion by 2015.

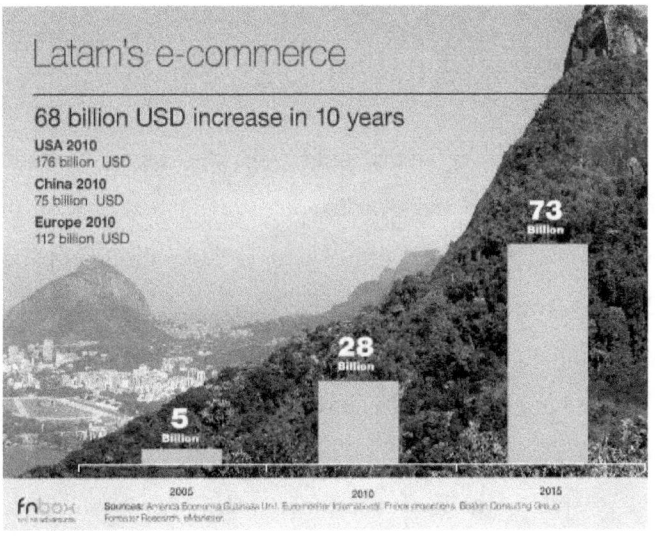

According to a report by the research firm Tendencias Digitales (2011), up to 60% of the online population in Latin America purchased goods online in the past year alone.

Consumers in Chile, Uruguay and Argentina are among the most prolific online buyers in the region. More than 50% of the Mexicans and Chileans prefer international ecommerce sites over local ones (comScore).

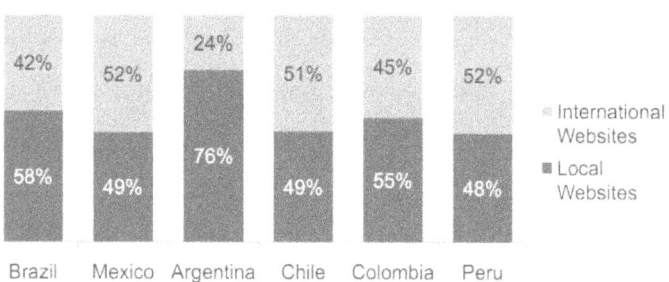

The most bought items online in the region include entertainment and travel tickets accounting for 31% of all products bought online. Other items include computer parts (23%), accessories and apparels (23%) and books (17%). According to eMarketer data, businesses to consumer are estimated to grow to $ 29 billion in 2015.

The vast majorities of consumers who visit ecommerce platforms will make a purchase online. However, retailers are facing an uphill task converting consumers to become actual online buyers. This can be attributed to online security concerns, limited selection of online products as well as inadequate payment options. While the region presents lucrative opportunity for growth, ecommerce in Latin America is still an infant industry. Nevertheless, consumers are showing a growing interest in online shopping with an average of 3 consumers out of 5 visiting ecommerce sites monthly.

Female web users are more prolific compared to males when it comes to online shopping. Brazil demonstrates the highest conversion rates from online ecommerce visitors to actual buyers, with up to 94% of site visitors making a purchase. Argentina and Columbia also have high conversion rates of up to 89% and 84% respectively.

Security is a major concern for web users who may be interested in online shopping, pushing potential ecommerce customers to brick-and-mortar stores instead. The payment options and shipping costs are also a significant hindrance for customers who are looking to adopt online shopping. According to comScore, consumers in Argentina show a greater propensity for shopping from local online sites than from international ones. This trend is the same in Brazil and Columbia, while a majority of online consumers in Mexico, Peru and Chile prefer to shop from international ecommerce sites as opposed to local ones. Overall, the import duty and taxes imposed on goods shopped online from international sites are steep across the region.

Credit card penetration in Latin America is significantly low, in contrast to the U.S. and Western Europe. Cash payment is the most preferred method of payment given the inadequate credit card infrastructure in the region. This is also attributable to the online security concerns that most people have. A majority of the countries in Latin America use the *Peso* as their primary currency while others like Brazil use the Real and the Venezuelans use Bolivars. While PayPal is an acceptable form of payment for online shopping in the region, it only accounts for 4.4% of all online payments, according to PlaySpan.

In the region, debit cards are more popular than credit cards. This is attributable to the high transaction costs involved in using credit cards, in contrast to other Western countries. Wire transfer is gaining greater acceptance in Latin America although some countries limit the amounts that can be transferred on any given day.

However, more players are coming into the ecommerce platform and advanced methods of payment such as

SafetyPal and Google Wallet are emerging. Mobile payments are also becoming a widely acceptable form of payment.

The growth of ecommerce in Latin America may be attributed to:

a) The emergence of new and safe mode of online payment methods allowing consumers to utilize both debit and credit cards for online shopping.

b) Increased efforts to boost online security; this has allowed more consumers to become confident about engaging in online shopping.

c) A growing number of online retailers offer a wider selection of goods and developing innovative methods of engaging with their customers.

The growth of m-commerce has boosted the ease with which consumers can buy and make payments online. This is attributable to unhindered penetration of smartphones in Latin America.

Argentina: Data from the Argentine Chamber of Ecommerce shows that the total sales from ecommerce in the past year (2011) were $2.6 million. This is projected to grow to $3.5 million at the end of 2012. In Argentina, the most purchased products include smartphones, adult clothing, home appliances and decoration as well as car accessories. Argentina leads Latin America in reach of coupon sites.

Brazil: Accounts for 70% of the online retail activity in Latin America. According to the research company E-bit, sales from ecommerce in Brazil averaged $19 billion in the past year (2011) and in the same year, there were up to 9 million new consumers making online purchases. Most of these new consumers were from the middle and emerging social economic classes in the country. Most online consumers in Brazil bought appliances, followed by computers, health and beauty products as well clothing and accessories. Mercado Libre is the most engaging online retail destination with 36 pages per visitor according to comScore.

Mexico: In 2011, the total ecommerce sales in Mexico amounted to $3.7 million according to the Mexican Internet Association. This is a 28% growth from the previous year. In Mexico, travel and entertainment tickets were the most purchased items online.

Columbia: The ecommerce sales in Columbia totaled 1.2 million in 2011 according to data from the Columbian Chamber of Ecommerce. This total is projected to grow by 100% by the end of 2012 to account for 2 billion.

In Puerto Rico, Ecuador, Panamá, Costa Rica and the Dominican Republic, the products that are popularly purchased include apparels, mobile phones, broadband services and computers.

8

Online Marketing In Australia And New Zealand

The markets in Australia and New Zealand are developed in terms of Internet technology and purchasing power. More than 85% of the population of Australia and New Zealand (20 million users) is online. Unlike other areas of the Asia Pacific, Australia and New Zealand do not pose any significant language barriers. This makes these two countries lucrative markets for businesses that are looking to expand into the region. Here are some considerations for businesses looking to expand into Australia and New Zealand:

Cultural Differences: Dos And Don'ts

When doing business and marketing to Australia and New Zealand, it is important that you take into consideration the business culture. Some factors to consider are:

Unlike Asians who seek to establish a relationship before getting to core business, Australians prefer to get straight to the point. They are also straightforward in their communication and will say 'no' or 'yes' when the occasion calls for it, unlike the Asians who do not always say 'no.' So, go ahead and send out your core message when you have an audience.

Humor is an important aspect of Australian communication. Including humor in your marketing messages may help, but be sure not to offend any ethnic groups or market segment.

While there may be space for lengthy negotiation with Asians, Australians do not spend too much time negotiating or bargaining. Ensure that your first proposed price is suitable and will not require bargaining.

The Australians do not work well with hard selling techniques. They typically take time to come to decisions; decisions are usually made after consulting with subordinates and top-level decision makers. Thus, you might have to demonstrate patience especially when you are involved in business-to-business marketing.

As you market your brand and product offering, refrain from hype and pompous claims about your brand or product. The Australians are more impressed by data than emotions.

The Kiwis (New Zealanders) are generally reserved and may hesitate to engage with people (or brands) that they are unfamiliar with. However, they are sociable once they establish a relationship with you. You must give them a reason to trust you.

As you market to this target audience, do not come out too forward or try to be overtly friendly. They particularly appreciate a sense of humor and ethics. If they perceive your business is unethical, this could significantly harm your business and marketing efforts in the country.

As in Australia, decision-making takes time. Thus, refrain from hard selling and pressurizing buyers. Clearly show the value of your product instead of being theoretical about this value or benefit. Consider that Kiwis are less inclined to bargain over price and instead they look out for the product that offers value for money. As you market your product, be careful not to go overboard and to oversell. New Zealanders are wary of people who engage in high selling techniques and those who cannot keep their word.

Because people in New Zealand appreciate honesty and ethical dealings, be sure to make your proposals and customer agreements transparent and clear to all parties.

Website Design And Customer Engagement

Admittedly, the audience in Australia and New Zealand has similarity with that in North America and Europe. Some website design considerations to make include:

Speak the appropriate lingo: The local dialects are very particular to both Australians and New Zealanders. This will certainly require some research on your side or work with a native to create content that appeals to the local dialects of these two countries.

Clarify your audience: ensure that your target audience knows what your site offers as soon as they visit it. Make your website easy to find and to access information. This calls for a less cluttered site and one that is straight to the point. If you are a business from overseas, tell your audience where you are from and what your brand is about.

Australia has specific domain registration regulations. You must register your company in Australia to use the '.com.au' or '.net.au' domains. The domain name you choose should have a strong correlation with the represented business.
The '.org.au' and 'asn.au' domains are reserved for non-profits organizations and must also have strong and direct

connection to the represented organization. On the other hand, the id.au is reserved for individual users who live in Australia.

The Australian and New Zealand audience is inclined to simple and easy to follow websites. Thus, make the navigation easy, use few images and include precise but adequate content on your sites. As with other Western cultures, it is best to stick with neutral colors, such as blue when designing the website.

Search Engine Marketing (SEO & PPC)

In Australia, SEO demonstrates its own uniqueness that local businesses may be more aware of than their foreign counterparts. One of this is the use of colloquialism and slang when communicating with the Australian audience. The Australians utilize a different language and their spellings are significantly different when looking up for a product or brand online. Thus, as a marketer, you must take into consideration the local language, slang and idioms when selecting keywords for your SEO campaign. It may be beneficial to work with a local SEO company to really understand the language nuances in the country.

National holidays and culture play an important role in Australia. When creating copy and optimizing your website landing pages, it is worthwhile to take into consideration these special occasions. This is particularly important when creating an ecommerce site for this audience. Some important holidays include 'Melbourne Cup', the 'Queen's birthday', 'Australia Day', 'ANZAC Day' and 'Labor Day'. Tourism is also an important part of the Australian society. By targeting these special occasions and cultural factors, you will be in a better position to reach your target audience and to make profits in the process.

Link building for your Australian website may also have its own unique considerations. Thus, it may be beneficial to work with a local agency that is aware of high-ranking websites that you should seek to link to.

To obtain a top-level domain such as '.com.au', your business should be registered in the country upon which you will be issued an Australian business number. It is important to have the '.com.au' domain; this will go a long way in optimizing your site for local search. Additionally, it is advisable that you host your website locally. Previously, search engine spiders would only crawl top-level domains to determine the website location. Today, the search engine algorithms also consider the Internet provider (IP) to determine the location of a website and to rank it appropriately for local search.

In New Zealand, the domain name is equally an important feature of site optimization. To become visible in the local search, your website should appear as a site located in New Zealand. People are also more likely to click through to your site if they perceive that website is locally based. As such, choose a domain name that includes .nz and ensure that the website is hosted within the country. As seen, local hosting can have an impact on your local search rankings.

Additionally, not all web users are aware of google.co.nz search and they are more likely to simply use google.com. However, google.com will not offer results that are specifically related to services in New Zealand unless the user includes 'New Zealand' or 'NZ' in their search. As such, it is essential that you optimize your website for keywords that will generate results specific to services and products offered in New Zealand. A simple way to do this is to include the 'NZ' or 'New Zealand' as part of your key phrases.

It is important to note that NZ and New Zealand will not generate the same results because these are different searches. As such, use both terms in your optimization campaign to allow your site to rank well on both fronts.

The major search engines in Australia and New Zealand and their market share, courtesy of Experian Hitwise, are:

In Australia
Google: 69% market share
Yahoo: 17% market share
Microsoft: 7% market share
Ask: 3% market share
AOL: 3% market share

In New Zealand
Google Nz: 86% market share
Google.com: 7%
Bing: 2.20%
Nz Yahoo search: 1.1%
Yahoo: 1%

While many companies globally have become increasingly aware of search engine and the marketing potential it holds, Australia still lags behind when compared to countries in

Western Europe and North America. Even though some companies use SEO as part of their marketing strategies, many more do not use these techniques.

Up to 90% of Australian Internet users utilize search engines to look for websites, products and services. Google accounts for a large share of the search market, more so for the fact that it was the first to offer Australian targeted search results. Presently, SEO services and pay-per-click campaigns are still relatively affordable in the country, offering a lucrative opportunity for businesses looking to fully utilize search engines for their marketing efforts.

In New Zealand, the search marketing trends are almost similar to those in Australia. Recent research by IAB New Zealand shows that businesses and marketers are investing more in display advertising and online classifieds part of their marketing campaigns. Unlike global trends where search engine marketing has increased in popularity, these trends are yet to catch up in New Zealand. Search marketing spending in Australia is about 46%, 57% in the UK and 41% in United States. However, the market share for search engine marketing in New Zealand stands at 25% while online classifieds and display advertising account for 44% and 31% respectively.

One of the reasons why search advertising and online advertising in general is still lagging behind in New Zealand may be a lack of sophistication and savvy on the part of businesses. Other than the travel industry, search marketing is still underdeveloped in the country but this offers an opportunity for early adopters and savvy marketers to leverage the market while it is still unsaturated and generally less costly.

Social Media Marketing

In New Zealand, social networking is the most popular online activity, according to a recent survey by comScore. Social networking engagements account for up to 22% of activities in the country. Engagement with portals such as Yahoo is the second most popular online activity for Kiwis, accounting for up to 14%.

The comScore survey also showed that although both males and females use social media almost equally, females are more engaged and spend more time on social networking sites compared to male users. Additionally female users are 15% more inclined to view pages on social network sites while male users are 16% less inclined to view these pages.

According to studies by Experian Hitwise there is a decline in the number of users visiting Bebo. For a long time, Bebo was the most popular social networking site in New Zealand, but Facebook and YouTube penetration has overtaken Bebo. In fact, in just the past two years since 2010, Facebook's traction in New Zealand has grown by up to 72%. However, while Facebook continues to attract a large percentage of social media users, Bebo has its own loyal following - notably the Pacific Islanders and Maoris.

Interestingly social networking sites attract more visits from less affluent users such mosaic groups, families living on low-income, those living in the urban suburbs and young city dwellers. This trend has made it difficult to monetize social networking platforms. As such, marketers need to think twice about using social media as a primary method of engaging with the audience in New Zealand.

YouTube and Facebook are increasingly attracting clicks. More and more users seem to migrate from Bebo to Facebook. Twitter and YouTube are also becoming popular and are rapidly attracting new visitors.

According to a study by TNS Digital Life, up to 54% of users in New Zealand are uninterested in engaging with a brand through social media. 67% of those interviewed report that they only join a brand community on social media to take advantage of a special offer but were not looking for a long-term social media engagement with the brand. Most customers refrain from this type of engagement to avoid receiving too many brand messages. As such, it is important that brands looking to engage with social media users offer relevant content and messages to really draw in this target audience.

While significant majorities of Kiwis do not want to engage with a brand through social media, consumers often use social media platforms for brand recommendations and to read reviews by other consumers before making a purchasing decision. The study by Digital Life indicates that Kiwis spend a large amount of their online time (39%) looking for information related to pre-purchases.

According to a Nielsen report, web users in Australia are widely receptive of social media. Users are increasingly utilizing social media as a source of information as well as a communication tool. 1 out of every 4 minutes online by Australians are spent on social networking sites. Up to 43% of social media users, utilized these platforms to offer reviews about a product and up to 74% of users utilize social media to read reviews about brands and products. Up to 42% of users have engaged with a brand through social media and 15% frequently do so. 46% of social media users have 'Liked' a brand on Facebook.

Social media networks market share in New Zealand:
Facebook: 4.9% market share and 82% reach
YouTube: 3.64% market share and 70% reach
Linkedin: 15% reach
Tagged: 0.44% market share
Twitter: 0.18% market share and 27% reach
MySpace: 0.10% market share and 36% reach
Windows Live Home: 0.07% market share
Zwinky: 0.006% market share
eBuddy: 0.05% market share
Small Worlds: 0.04% market share
Meebo: 0.03% market share

According to the Australia Bureau of statistics (2011), Facebook is the most dominant social media network in the country with close to 10 million active users. This accounts for 65% of social media market share in the country.

Interestingly, StumbleUpon is also widely used in the country, with figures from Stat Counter showing that it accounts for 12% of the social media platform. Google's social network, Google +1 is more popular in Australia than it is globally.

Social media networks market share in Australia according to Google DoubleClick Ad Planner Tool:

Facebook: 9.8 million unique visitors (UV) each month

Youtube: 6.7 million UV

Blogspot: 2.2 million UV

Twitter: 1 million UV

WordPress: 920,000 UV

LinkedIn: 760,000 UV

MySpace: 630,000 UV

Flickr: 630,000 UV

Tumblr: 350,000 UV

Digg: 110,000 UV

StumbleUpon: 94,000 UV

Reddit: 57,000 UV

Delicious: 52,000 UV

83% of the small Australian businesses have a Facebook page, 27% a Twitter account and 20% a Linkedin profile (AIMIA). Businesses use social media sites:

a)   as a two-way communication with their customers

b)   to collect reviews and online comments

c)   and to offer incentives.

	Small	Medium	Large
Facebook page	83%	79%	82%
Twitter	27%	33%	71%
LinkedIn	20%	20%	30%
Google+	8%	5%	11%
Youtube	4%	5%	29%
Blog	4%	6%	13%

Email Marketing

Email Marketing is the most used online marketing channel in Australia and New Zealand followed by Search Engine Optimization (SEO). There are strict laws that govern email marketing in New Zealand, to mitigate the problem of email spamming. Marketers are required to obtain permission from users in the form of opt-ins before sending them emails. Consent to receive emails may be direct when the recipient sends a message allowing you to send them emails.

Consent may also be implied, when a relationship between the consumer and marketer already exists.

The regulations prohibit the sending of unsolicited emails that feature a New Zealand link. It is also required that marketers include adequate and factual information about the recipient of the email and easily allow him or her to opt-out. It is prohibited to use software that collects people's addresses without their consent.

In Australia, the same regulations apply with regard to sending unsolicited emails. Email usage is noticeably more prevalent in Australia than it is New Zealand.

According to the Australian Communication and Media authority, most Australians have more than one email addresses that they use for different purposes including for work, school and home uses. Mobile phones with Internet access have made it easier for people in the country to access email. The ACMA reports that up to 64% of users with 3G mobile devices used their phones to access email. This means that the opening rate for emails has grown thereby enabling users to engage with brands faster and frequently. It is beneficial for marketers to employ resources that will enable them to monitor how customers are reacting to an email campaign.

The study by ACMA also shows that web hosted emails such as Gmail are increasingly popular accounting for 68% of email services market share. Marketers should take into consideration that every web-hosted application for email would display their HTML email differently. Carrying out email testing can help to determine the look of your emails in the widely used web email applications in this region.

Mobile Marketing

Mobile marketing involves the use of mobile phone technology to send promotional messages directly to mobile phone users. This includes advertising within applications or sending SMS notifications. Mobile marketing is becoming a significant part of marketing campaigns given the sheer mobile phone penetration globally. Other newer forms of mobile marketing include:

The use of location base services for example FourSquare: This entails determining the location of your target audience and then sending them promotional messages related to businesses in that geographical location.

Augmented reality: These mobile campaigns entail displaying location specific details about a business and its service/product offering on a phone user's phone interface.

Two-dimensional bar codes for example QR codes: These are essentially mobile forms of barcodes that a mobile user can scan to access specific information about a business and its product offering.

GPS messaging: Entails sending location specific messages that appear on a user's mobile phone when they enter a certain geographical range.

The ACMA reports that in Australia the number of people who own a standard mobile phone has reduced over the years, while those who own iPhones and other types of smart phones has increased. The most popular mobile handset is Nokia accounting for 41% of the market share followed by Apple at 21%, Samsung at 12% and Blackberry at 3%. Up to 9% of mobile phone users, primarily use their phones for banking at least once each month. 10% of those surveyed use their mobile phones for online shopping

Presently, there are approximately 10 million smartphone users in Australia. Smartphone penetration in the region is the second highest in Australia at 52% of the population, after Singapore whose smart phone penetration is at 62%. In Australia 49% of the smartphone users have an iPhone while in New Zealand only 32%.

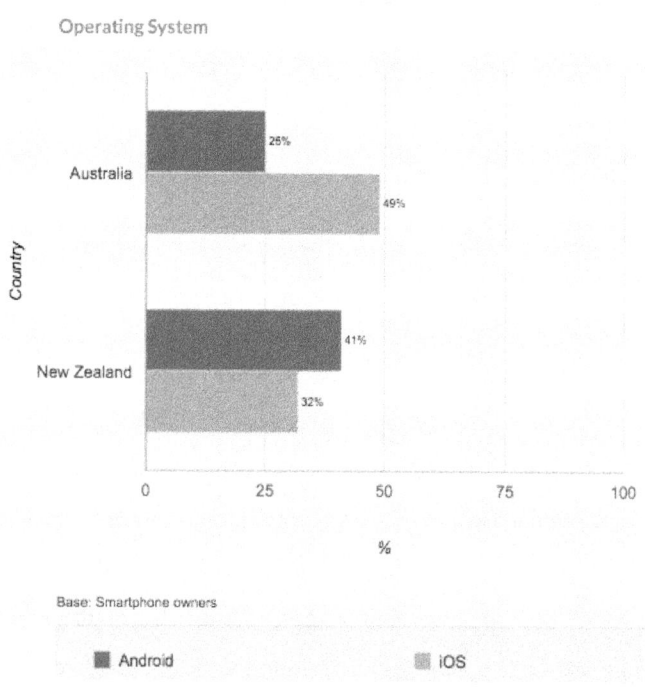

Operating System

Base: Smartphone owners

Both males and females in the country use their mobile devices at an equal rate, most of them spending most of their mobile Internet time searching for information and accessing email. Marketers should consider investing in mobile ads including AdWords and iAd, social media marketing, and geo-location services such as Foursquare.

A study by inMobi (2011) showed that Australians were amenable to mobile ads than users in North America and Asia. At least 75% of those surveyed were contented about receiving mobile ads on their phones, compared to 63% and 69 % of North Americans and Asians. The study also shows that Australians are generally less receptive to Internet ads and more accepting of mobile ads even though they do have access to computers and Internet connectivity.

In New Zealand, the smart phone penetration is at 30%, but this is expected to rise to account for 50% of mobile devices. This rise in smartphone penetration in the country is attributable to the falling costs of data and handsets, according to an Interactive Advertising Bureau (IAB), NZ Mobile Advertising Council (MAC) and 3DI survey. When compared to Australia, the smartphone penetration in New Zealand is lower. There are more than 5 million mobile phone users in the country but just a few actually own a smart phone.

Android smart phones have greater popularity (50%) than regular phones (39%) in New Zealand. Up to 30% of users in the country are receptive to mobile ads compared to 75% of Australian mobile phone users. Those who have smartphones have up to 10 mobile applications but use just three or five at most, daily.

Kiwis frequently switch between different forms of media with as many as 64% reporting that they use their phones while watching television and using their computers. A majority of smartphone owners use their phones to access emails, browsing the net, making phone calls and utilizing applications. Unlike their Australian counterparts, Kiwis are less likely to do online shopping. In both Australia and New Zealand, pay as you go subscriptions are more popular.

Affiliate Marketing

Affiliate marketing has been thrust to the forefront in both Australia and New Zealand given the global recession, which has seen more and more people looking for discounted products, making affiliate marketing a viable channel for ecommerce merchants.

Affiliate marketing in New Zealand is catching up, even though it is not as extensively developed as it is in North America or Western Europe. The model is in fact attractive to the typical New Zealander who is looking to make some extra money on the side.

In both countries, affiliate marketing primarily falls into categories such as voucher code sites for example freecouponcodes.com in New Zealand; cash-back platforms such as Fonzii, paid search affiliates, content affiliate marketing and email affiliate marketing.

As with their Asian counterparts, affiliate marketers (especially in New Zealand) are more receptive to local affiliate networks than global ones. Some local ones include Prints, Elldridge Lynth, Real Groovy and iSubscribe among others.

Affiliate marketing in Australia is more established than it is in New Zealand with global networks such as ClickBank and Amazon Affiliates accounting for a significant share of the affiliate market in the country. Other popular networks include Commission Monster, Commission Factory, Clixgalore among others.

Video Marketing

Video marketing entails the use of video sharing platforms such as YouTube to market a brand and its product offering.

Video marketing is based on the premise that target audiences are more inclined to view a video than they are to read a textual message. Video marketing is also effective due to the share-ability of videos and the viral effect that this sharing can attract.

According to Internet World Stats (2011) there are up to 4 million Internet users in New Zealand, accounting for 85% of the country's online population. comScore (2011) reports that up to 2.1 million Internet users in the country view online video, accounting for 77% of the country's online population. In Australia there are 1bn videos watched every month.

In New Zealand, Google Sites is the most popular platform for video viewing, accounting for 1.7 million viewers who viewed up to 81.6 million videos. Google Sites is primarily supported by YouTube, which accounts for up to 52% of all the online videos viewed in the country. Vevo attracts an estimated 400,000 viewers, while local video platforms TVNZ and MediaWorks account for an estimated 201,000 and 150,000 viewers respectively. Both male and female users aged between 15 and 34 years were the most engaged with online videos.

More than three quarters of the online population in Australia view video content via a computer at least once each month. Meanwhile 26% of the online population view online videos using their mobile phones. According to a Nielsen report (2011) video consumers in the country consume up to 8 hours of online video with male users spending more time with online videos than female users.

An increasing number of businesses are investing a significant amount of their advertising budget in online video marketing. The real estate industry has extensively embraced the potential of video marketing; real estate listings with a video are receiving more inquires than those that do not have videos. Buyers are using digital media as part of their research before making a final buying decision. Buyers are also sharing the content that they access online, leading to greater exposure for businesses that have embraced video marketing in the country. In addition to the real estate sector, sectors such as finance, leisure, tourism and health are increasingly incorporating video into their e- marketing strategy.

Ecommerce

Australia and New Zealand present a lucrative market for ecommerce. The online population is looking to engage with brands that offer value and that can be trusted. As indicated earlier, a large majority of consumers does not expect to haggle over prices and are instead looking for a provider who offers value for money. Unlike in Europe and Asia where language fragmentation poses a significant barrier, general language uniformity in both Australia and New Zealand opens up more channels for ecommerce.

According to IBM (2012), online spending in Australia increased by 12% in the past two years. Online shoppers spent up to $12 billion in the surveyed years (2010-2012). Research companies Frost & Sullivan indicated that Internet shopping spends will increase to $18 billion by 2014. Amazon is the top retail site and more than 75% of the Australian retailers have an online presence. The average Australian online shoppers spend an average of $2,000 per year. 1 in 5 online Australian online shoppers purchased from overseas.

The 2012 Smarter Consumer Study by IBM shows that Australians are leading in acquiring new methods of online shopping. Up to 17% of those interviewed report that they are comfortable using more than one type of technology while shopping online. The study further shows that 90% of online shoppers in the country attribute their shopping decisions to social networks, while 40% of online shoppers compare different websites before making a final purchasing decision.

After looking for local information on a smartphone, in both Australia and New Zealand people take actions such as calling the business (more than 50%), visit the local business or their site (more than 50%), look up on a map (more than 40%) or make a purchase online (30%) (Our Mobile Planet).

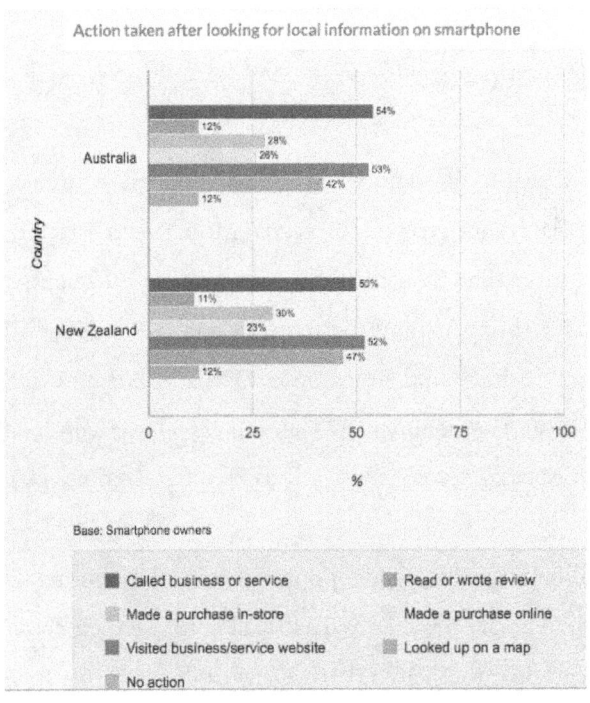

Action taken after looking for local information on smartphone

Base: Smartphone owners

- Called business or service
- Made a purchase in-store
- Visited business/service website
- No action
- Read or wrote review
- Made a purchase online
- Looked up on a map

The most preferred method of payment for online shopping in Australia is PayPal. According to the National Statistics Office, up to 30% of online shoppers are comfortable paying with PayPal while just 25% and 14% use Visa and MasterCard respectively. Like Kiwis, Australian online shoppers purchase most of their online merchandise from international sites but are less willing to use their credit cards on these sites.

Popular ecommerce sites in Australia include:
Ebay: 5.18%
Gumtree: 1.51%
Harvey Norman: 0.49%

In New Zealand, the number of online shoppers continues to show significant growth. According to a Nielsen report, there are more than 2 million online shoppers in the country. Most online shoppers purchase travel tickets (50%), followed by apparels, shoes and accessories (32%), magazines and books (29%), entertainment (27%) and travel services such as hotel bookings (24%).

At least half of the online population in the country is comfortable to shop online and are willing to use their credit cards, according to Nielsen data. Daily deals platforms such as TreatMe and GrabOne are the most frequently visited sites. The wide accessibility of debit cards and social media reviews is seeing more shoppers opt for online shopping rather than shop in retail stores.

Not only are more people buying online, they are also purchasing more. Kiwis are also increasingly willing to buy from international sites with some online consumers reporting that it is cheaper for them to purchase on international websites than it is from local ones. This can be attributed to the increase in goods on sales tax imposed on online shoppers who buy locally. Purchases as small as $400 do not attract import taxation. TradeMe is the most popular ecommerce platform. Others include eStaronline and Direct Payment Solutions.

The National Statistics Office in New Zealand indicates that the use of credit cards for payment was at 63% as of 2011. There number of credit card transactions in the country has risen significantly.

According to the Lafferty Group World Cards Intelligence data, Kiwis are the most prolific users of credit cards for making online payment. They use credit cards for everyday purchases rather than for just major purchases such as vacations or cars. The amount of credit card spend in the country averages $7,300. Overall, debit cards and credit cards are widely used for both offline and online payments. Prepaid cards are also widely popular among New Zealanders including gift cards, travel cards and reloadable cards.

Alibaba in Australia

In Australia, Alibaba is gaining considerable traction with more than 500,000 Australian users utilizing the platform as a source of business merchandise. There are also more than 20,000 Australian users visiting and using the site each month.

Australia is becoming one of the largest markets for Alibaba globally, overtaking the U.S. and Britain. The popularity of Alibaba in Australia can be attributed to the growth of the ecommerce industry in the country. An increasing number of small and medium enterprises are looking to source for products and services overseas. Up to 87% of local businesses are using Alibaba to source for products and services with most of them sourcing clothing and shoes, machinery, computers, vehicles and home appliances and products.

Taxation and Tariffs

In New Zealand, online purchases attract a goods and services tax (GST) of up to 15% as well as import duty. The import duty will vary with the type of purchase; duty is generally imposed on goods that are already manufactured in the country. This aims to protect local businesses and industry. Books, Videos and CDS, Watches, computers and computer games do not incur duty. Apparels and shoes purchased overseas incur up to 10% of import duty and GST. The customs officials generally do not charge GST and import duty for goods that may attract less than NZ$60; this only applies to non-alcoholic and non-tobacco products. In Australia now, no GST (goods and service tax) is incurred on goods that are bought from international ecommerce sites for less than $1000.

9

Online Marketing In Middle East And North Africa

The Internet market in the Middle East and North Africa (MENA) region is much larger than most people outside the region may know. Although this is a largely conservative region compared to Western standards, plenty of research indicates that the Arabic region is becoming more prolific in terms of ecommerce and Internet usage. The number of web users is estimated to grow to 82 million in the coming years. People in this region spend online more than 3 hours every day and the Arabic language is the fastest growing language online.

The MENA region presents a promising opportunity for Internet marketing and global ecommerce given that it is an unsaturated market for now. A survey by Visa released at the end of 2011 shows that online retail in the region is at a peak in part due to the availability of disposable income as well as an increase in credit card penetration. In fact, up to 77 million users in the regions are looking for products on the Internet and are specifically leveraging the variety offered by online stores. A study by Effective Measure & Spot On PR, up to 34% of Internet users in the MENA region are purchasing products and services from the Internet. This trend is led by the Gulf countries of Saudi Arabia, Qatar, UAE, Oman, Kuwait and Bahrain.

The MENA market can be geographically categorized into five regions:

North Africa: Egypt, Tunisia, Morocco, Libya and Algeria

Central region: Palestine, Jordan, Lebanon and Syria

Arab Gulf: Saudi Arabia, Oman, Kuwait, the United Arab Emirates, Qatar and Bahrain

Eastern region: Iraq and Iran

Central Region: Palestine, Syria, Lebanon and Jordan

The highest Internet Penetration in the region is seen in countries such as UAE (3,5 million online users), Bahrain (700,000 online users), Kuwait (1,1 million online users), Quatar (563,000 online users), Morocco (16 million online users), Saudi Arabia (11 million online users) and Egypt (22 million online users (samer-baydoun.com).

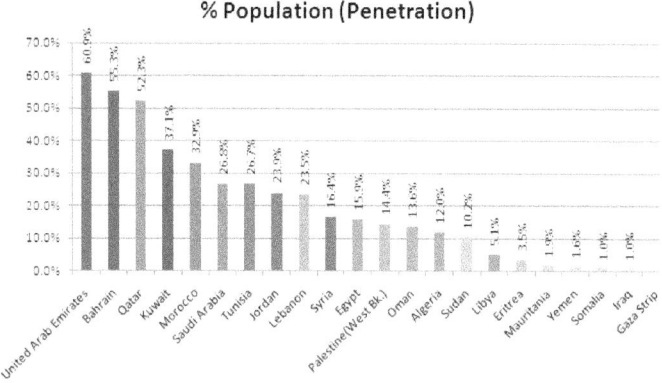

% Population (Penetration)

The Arabic Gulf region hosts the high net consumers or the affluent Middle Class. It is a region that is significantly wealthier than the rest of the region and features higher Internet penetration, online shopping and credit card usage trends that can be compared with Western trends. This market generally has a high disposable income, a high purchasing power, hosts a large group of expatriates and highly skilled workers.

Cultural Differences Do's And Dont's

From a foreigner's point of view, the MENA region can be associated with a lot of myths and stereotypes. Approaching this region with misconceived presumption can make it difficult to market and do business here. It is important to approach the region with an open mind and to familiarize yourself with the actual business and societal culture to ensure success in your online marketing efforts in the region.

As with other regions in the world, it is imperative to take into consideration the differences between the countries in the MENA region. Even though a large majority of the people here are Arabs, there are cultural nuances that set each country apart. Approaching all countries, the same way might be perceived as a sign of ignorance. Admittedly, a common religion and language makes it easier to approach the region, but it is always a good idea to find out what sets one country apart from the other.

When marketing to the MENA region, consider the prayer routines of your audience. People will be less receptive to a marketing message during prayer time, especially on Fridays when congregational prayers are held.

Also, avoid carrying out business over the month of Ramadan as this is the fasting season for Muslims. Business hours are also largely constrained and people are likely to be less receptive over this period. Other important festivals to observe are 'Eid al Fitr' and 'Eid al Adha', which come after Ramadan and the annual pilgrimage respectively. If you are trying to collaborate with local partners for your online campaign, try not to do business around these holidays.

Generally, Arabs are less informal with names, when compared to cultures in the West. They prefer to go by the title and the first name. However bear in mind that women in this region will not post their pictures or identify themselves on a public site.

When collaborating with local partners for your campaign, you might find that the process of doing business is not linear or organized. Unlike in the West, the Arabs have a very thin line between business and personal spheres. Business is typically entangled with personal relationships, trust and family ties. It might take a while before your partners arrive at a decision. It is also important that you build a strong bond of trust before your audience can begin to do business with you.

Admittedly, the business atmosphere in the region revolves around favours. It pays off to have important contacts to get things done faster. It is commonplace for business partners to ask for favours and expect the same in return (the 'wasta' system).

Unlike in the West, people in the MENA region place more emphasis in what you say and not what you agree to on paper. While contracts are important, they only represent a memorandum of understanding rather than a sealed agreement. Thus, it is imperative that you promise only what you are capable of delivering; you will otherwise lose honour among your audience.

The initial meetings you have with any local partners are typically for establishing trust. Consider that solid relationships and trust are important factors for successfully doing business in the region. Unlike in the West where people tend to get straight to business, in the MENA region it is important that you take time to know each other first.

If you are engaged in any sort of negotiation with your audience, consider that Arabs do expect to negotiate and bargain. They are excellent at this. Unlike in some countries in the West for example in New Zealand and Australia where bargaining is not always expected, haggling is a common part of business in MENA. However, refrain from using high-pressure techniques when marketing to your audience; be patient!

Generally, people in this region are particularly proud of their language. It is good practice to learn a couple of Arabic words to start building important relationships with your audience. This will also show that you are as interested in the people as you are in doing business with them.

Finally, it is always a good idea to hire an intermediary to assist you in negotiations. Good places to look are local law firms with a good reputation or the local chambers of commerce.

Website Design And Customer Engagement

The MENA region can be significantly different from those in the West. Here are some factors to consider when designing a website targeting an Arab audience:

Collective culture: The MENA region demonstrates a collectivist culture in which community bonds are largely appreciated. As such, ensure that your website design emphasizes this community and familial bonding. Your audience is more likely to be attracted by a website that carries a family theme than one that revolves around an individual and his needs.

Gender roles: While masculinity may dominate the cultural landscape in the region, it is appropriate to include feminine elements into the website. Masculinity can be demonstrated through themes that emphasize success and status, products that are durable, and a feeling of enjoyment and escapade. On the other hand, femininity in a website can be demonstrated through softer topics and with a less aggressive selling approach.

High Context: The MENA region has a high context culture that values tradition and historical ties. As part of your website design for this audience, include themes that elucidate harmony, traditional values and history.

Power Distance: Honor, status and recognition are an important aspect of the Arabic culture. The region has a high power distance measure; a website that emphasizes honor and achievement is appropriate.

Spatial Orientation: Spatial orientation is the manner in which is displayed on a website. This can have a direct impact on user experiences, because it influences the visual appearance of the content and the website as a whole. By changing the spatial orientation, you can enhance the user experience, yet what is comfortable in one country may be different in another. Arabic is read from right to left, thus your website layout and spatial orientation must consider this. It is also a good idea to limit the usage of graphics, background music and pictures to those that will not provoke religious or political sentiments.

Domain name: One element of website localization is using a top level domain in each country involved in your online campaign for example for the United Arab Emirates the top level domain in .ae. It is also appropriate to use .com, .net, .org, .info and .biz. The hyphen (-) is used in Arabic domains to separate words.

Overall, an increasing number of webmasters are opting for Arabic URLs and non-ASCII characters to optimize websites for the Arabic language and audience. In addition, including Arabic keywords in the URLs and web page links will boost your site rankings on the search engines.

The use of Arabic domain names is fairly new. Many countries have now established services for pre-registering domain names. This is aimed at solving any challenges that may come about with the use of Arabic domain names as well as SEO key terms and phrases. Arabic domain names are an important step toward attaining high ranking and search results in the Arabic search engines.

While English is not the predominant business language in the region, many foreign companies looking to target the Arabic audience still offer their content only in English. It is a misconception to design your website content solely in English, thinking that this is an international business language. It is important that you enable your Arabic speaking audience to access web content in a language they are comfortable with.

Color considerations:

Green: symbolizes good fortune or holiness

Blue: is a color of protection and represents immortality

Yellow: demonstrates power, durability, wealth and happiness

Red: is symbolic of evil and danger

White: indicates mourning or pureness

Search Engine Marketing (SEO & PPC)

Research shows that most Arabic web users search using Arabic key terms to find accurate and relevant search results. This is particularly evident when the queries at search engines pertain to a country-specific topic. Web users also prefer to utilize Arabic search terms when looking for culture-specific information, local events, news as well as products and services that are particular to a country. As such, this calls for marketers to localize almost all of their web content in Arabic and to display an interface that is culturally fitting. Arabic is the 7th most spoken language online (after English, Chinese, Spanish, Japanese, Portuguese and German) and it is expected to rank 4th by 2015. Currently less than 2% of the online content is in Arabic. Arabic is the main language in the MENA region (23 countries) with the exception of Israel where they speak Hebrew.

The large majority of consumers in the MENA region do not speak English and in some countries such as Algeria, Morocco and Tunisia, they largely speak French. This further emphasizes the need to use Arabic when marketing to this region. It may be valuable to work with a local translation partner to localize your Arabic website and to create a website that takes into consideration the SEO nuances suitable for this market.

Working with a local translation and SEO partner in this region is important because:

a) There are six primary dialects in the region.

b) SEO in the region is unique and is underscored by the need to use varying keywords and tagging techniques for the different markets.

c) Some images may have offensive cultural suggestions that may not be apparent to a foreign marketer.

To choose the appropriate keywords and Meta tags for your Arabic web content, you require in-depth organic research on the chosen keywords. To make the most of your SEO campaign, it is imperative that you do not simply directly translate the keywords. Instead, a better approach is to develop proper Arabic key terms and phrases pertaining to your products/services. Google offers resources to look up for Arabic words, to locate related key terms and those key words that are popularly used to query Google search engines. Yamli.com and keyboard.org are two sites that translate English and French into Arabic while you type and you could use them when you start working on your keyword research.

Google has 15 domains in the Arabic countries and provides an English version only of the Egyptian and Saudi Arabian sites. There are more than 100 million searches made daily across the MENA region (54% of the searches are made in Arabic, 34% in English and 8% in French – Alexandra Tohme) with the biggest search category being news. 30% of the Google searches are local searches.

Your long-term SEO campaign in the region should entail the use of Arabic and English keywords as these are generally the main business languages in the region. Additionally, it is important to consider that there are different foreign markets or expatriates in areas such as the United Arab Emirates. These market segments are likely to search in their own language. If you are looking to target any of these expatriate groups, you should undertake research to find out the language they prefer to use when searching.

Undertaking online business in the MENA region may not be as successful if it is limited to a single culture or language. A better approach is to create bilingual web content to really cater to the dynamic differences in this market. As seen previously, search trends among web consumers in the region are largely based on the Arabic language but a majority of them can also read the English or French language. To ensure that your marketing campaign in the region meets its objective, consider the bilingual nature of your audience.

It is important for foreign marketers to pay attention to the search marketing requirements in each county. While you can decide to spend most of your marketing budget on online banners or use offline strategies for advertising, this might not be effective in the long term. Additionally, if you overlook the search trends in the region, it is likely that you will target only users who use either the traditional media or just online users. The point here is to optimize your online campaign by integrating it with suitable offline marketing strategies. This way, you are able to funnel a significant number of users to your site and to keep them engaged with your brand and product offering.

Search engine marketing in this region is more about using the correct key terms in your web content. Because you are offering multilingual content, consider that integrating keywords into a localized website is less about translation and more about multilingual search optimization. Picking and structuring the appropriate keywords will also influence your pay-per-click campaigns. In addition to choosing the right keywords, you also need to choose keywords that are specific to each market involved in your campaign.

Social Media Marketing

Digital marketing in the MENA region is booming in part due to the increasing usage of social media among web consumers. To be successful in social media marketing in the region, it is essential that your campaign revolve around the social language, social matters and social ideas that are prevalent in any given market.

Facebook is currently the most popular social media in the region. Trends indicate that up to 38,000 web consumers join the platform each day. However, when compared to the Facebook penetration rates in other regions globally, there is room for increased social media use in the Middle East and North Africa.

YouTube is also widely used among web consumers and approximately 100 million videos are viewed in the region every day, accounting for one hour of video uploads every minute. However, when compared to global averages (48 hours of video downloads each minute), user engagement is still low in the region.

Twitter engagement among brands is especially low, but web users are demonstrating an inclination to using Twitter for information sharing about brands and products. 50% of the Twitter users have purchased as a result of Twitter.

27% of the MENA's digital marketing budget is spent on social media and 1 in 3 people in the Middle East have four social media accounts (socialbakers). The following is a graphic showing the Social Media Penetration (Facebook, Twitter and Linkedin) in some of the most active Arabic countries online.

Figure 32: Penetration of Social Media Users in the Select Arab Countries (June 2012)

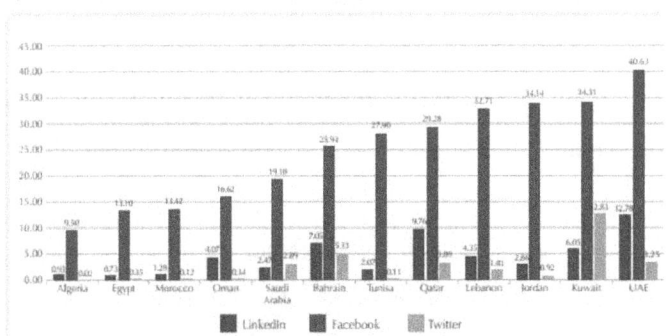

The MENA region represents 8% of the Facebook traffic. 88% of the Linkedin users in the MENA region are male (Arab Social Media Report) and the MENA region provides 3% of the Linkedin's total traffic. Turkey, Kuwait, Saudi Arabia, Quatar, Egypt and UAE lead the region for number of tweets and more than 60% of the tweets are in Arabic.

Study by TNS Digital shows the large majority of web consumers are using social media to spread the word about brands in an effort to help other consumers make informed purchasing decisions. This trend is particularly prevalent in Israel, Morocco, UAE and Saud Arabia. In these markets, up to 90% of online consumers report they trust the opinions of their online social networks with regard to brands and products. Additionally the Econsultancy Middle East and North Africa Digital Consumer Report shows that up to 79% of web uses in the region have 'liked' a brand on Facebook.

However, a recent poll by professional social networking platform, Bayt, shows that up to 48% of online consumers report that companies are not using social media appropriately. While up to 52% of companies in the region are using social media for marketing, a majority of users are apprehensive about the potential of social media to tarnish their reputation. Social media report that although companies have a presence on social media, they do engage enough with their target audience and failing to offer adequate feedback to inquiries made on social networks.

<u>Key findings in the report show that</u>:

In the first quarter of 2011, there were up to 28 million Facebook users in the MENA region. The average Facebook penetration was approximately 8%.

The countries in the Gulf Arab region are likely to dominate Facebook usage in the MENA region as a whole. Egypt hosts the highest number of Facebook users in the region, accounting for up to 2 million new users in the first quarter of 2011.

The most prolific Facebook users in the region are youth aged between 15 and 29 years, accounting for up to 70% of the Facebook population in the region. 60% of the Saudi Arabia Facebook accounts use Arabic as a communication language, 89% of the UAE use English and the 84% of the Maghreb countries use French (stateofsearch.com).

In the first quarter of 2011, the number of Twitter messages in the region had increased to 155 million daily, accounting for a 41% increase from the previous year.

There is also a 50% increase in Twitter signups using mobile phones. However, only an approximated 40 million Twitter users are actively engaged with the platform. This means that a small minority of Twitter users actually account for the information generated on this platform. The majority use Twitter more as a source of informant than a micro blogging platform for generating information.

Email Marketing

In the MENA region, digital marketing is flourishing according to a report by Econsultancy. The report shows that companies in the region are spending up to 22% of their marketing and advertising budgets on digital marketing, including email marketing and other forms of digital marketing.

The report shows that a large majority of companies in the region are leveraging email marketing. This can be attributed to the trends in the region in which email is the most popular online activity for web users in the region. Marketers in the region also prefer to use email for marketing because it is feasible to measure an email marketing campaign by monitoring the click through rates, the open rates and the number of un-subscription.

In spite of the fact that a large majority of users largely engage with email, marketers in the region are yet to apply best practices for email marketing. According to the research firm Real Opinions, consumers in the region report that the emails they receive from companies can serve to alienate them from the brand. According to the report, up to 32% of email recipients find the emails annoying even when recipients opted-in to receive the emails. This presents a challenge for marketers looking to leverage email to reach their audience in the region.

While the perceptions of emails from companies have declined globally, email marketing is an important feature of the marketing matrix for marketers in the MENA region. According to a recent report by the Forrester Research group:

The clicks through rates for emails are at 5% in contrast to online ad banners, which only receive an average click through rate of 2.5%.

Customers who purchase products advertised in emails are likely to spend up to 139% more than those who do not purchase through email marketing. The percentage of consumers who buy products advertised through emails, do so impulsively and buy on credit.

Almost half of email users who do not mind promotional emails report that emails are great for finding out about a product or special offers. These consumers are also willing to pay a premium price for a product that offers them convenience.

Email consumers who buy product marketed through emails are likely to offer a product review. This accounts for up to two thirds of email users. Another three quarters are likely to forward email ads to their friends and families.

To optimize their email marketing campaigns marketers are using CRM systems that allow them to better understand the needs of their target audience before sending out emails. It is worth noting that while digital marketing is thriving in the region, there is still a general lack of expertise when it comes to online marketing best practices. Marketers report that most companies in the region are still inclined to use traditional forms of marketing even when online marketing presents better opportunities. Other challenges that Internet marketers doing business in the region are likely to face with regard to email marketing are low broadband penetration as well as underdeveloped ecommerce infrastructure that may hinder customers from making online purchases.

Mobile Marketing

The recent *Our Mobile Planet smartphone research*, by Google Mobile Ads and Ipsis MediaCT conducted in the first quarter of 2012 shows that the MENA region is leading in smartphone penetration rates globally. There are up to 61% and 60% of smartphone users in the UAE and Saudi Arabia. In the UAE up to 72% of smartphone users are utilizing their devices to access Internet on a daily basis and the iPhone is the most operating system in the UAE and Saudi Arabia.

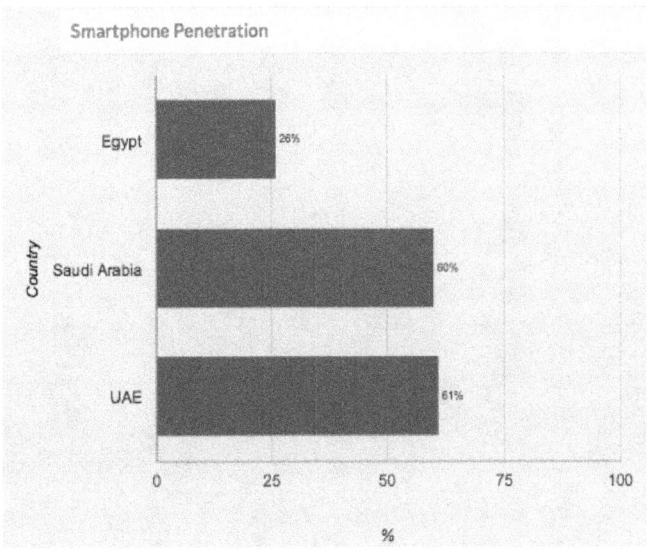

General Smartphone Activities

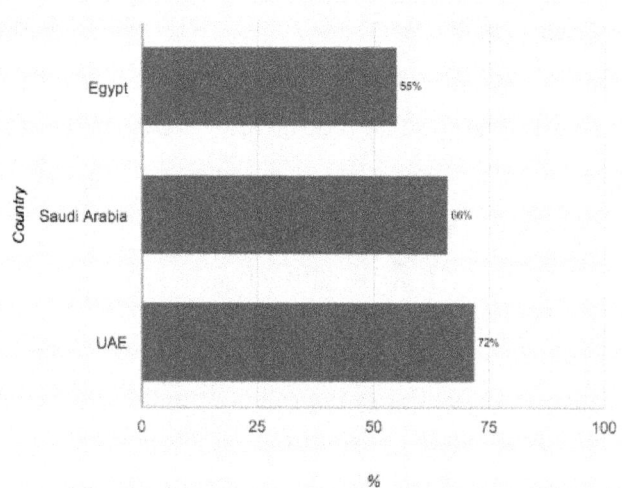

Operating System

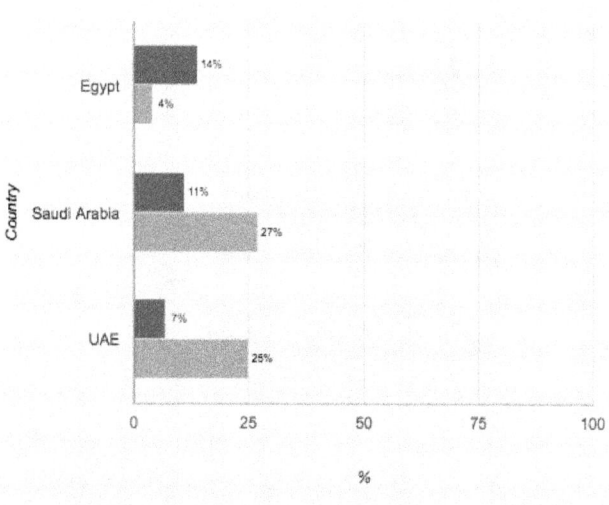

Base: Smartphone owners

Android   iOS

The region hosts young mobile shoppers and social network users. The study shows that large markets such as Egypt, Saudi Arabia and UAE have a high percentage of young, male smartphone users, with males aged below 34 years accounting for up to 72% of the smartphone user population.

Additionally, smartphone users are also the most prolific shoppers in the region. In Egypt up to 42% of smartphone users have bought something online using their smartphone. 80% of these mobile shoppers make at least one purchase each month.

In addition to mobile shopping, a large majority of smartphone users are using their mobile devices to interact with online and offline ads. For example, more than three quarters of smartphone users in Egypt used their phones to find a company online after seeing a commercial on TV. In fact, up to 90% of smartphone users in the UAE, Saudi Arabia and Egypt take note of mobile ads as they search the web with their mobile devices.

Key findings of the Google research show that:

a) Smartphone users largely used their mobile devices to view news, access information and email and to participate in social networking.

b) More than half of those who participated in the survey report that they access websites and apps from their smart phones at least once each day.

c) The UAE has the highest number of app downloads, accounting for up to 50% of those interviewed. Up to 49% downloaded free apps and 27% have up to five paid apps.

d) Over half of those interviewed preferred cash on delivery instead of using credit card payments through their mobile phones.

In Saudi Arabia, which is the largest, and one of the richest countries in the region, up to 47% of smartphone users have a data plan for their mobile phones. Unlike in the West and specifically in the U.S. where mobile usage is higher among the young population, in countries such as Saudi Arabia, the elderly are more prolific in their mobile phone usage. In this market, up to 42% of smartphone users use their mobile devices to access information and local news and up to 29% use their devices to download applications.

Up to 52% of smartphone users in Saudi Arabia use their phones to visit mobile websites and access applications multiple times each day. While males access news and information frequently on their smartphones, women engage with social networks more.

Another large market is Egypt in which more smartphone users have mobile data plans, when compared to users in Saudi Arabia. Up to 32% of users in Egypt use mobile apps, 45% utilize their mobile browsers while up to 62% of user utilize their smartphone more than once each day. Access to news, information, email and social media are the most common mobile activity for users in this region.

In the UAE, the financial capital of the MENA region and home to one of the wealthiest cities in the world, Dubai, up to 56% of smart phone users have mobile data plans across all ages above 19 years. Up to 45% of users access news and information, while 44% and 39% use their smartphones to access email and social networks respectively.

A prevalent alternative to data plans for smartphones is pre-paid mobile plans. While pre-paid is not the dominant data plans for users in Western Europe and North America, most mobile phone usage in the world is powered by pre-paid plans.

Affiliate Marketing

Affiliate marketing also known as performance based marketing or cost per action, is yet to thrive in the Middle East and North Africa region. This can be attributed in part to the fact that over the past years, regional portals affiliated with mainstream media networks with a lot of resources for advertising and content development have dominated the market. These established website have been using CPM campaigns to funnel general and less targeted traffic to their site while at the same time selling their ad space based on CPM as well.

Companies looking to roll out affiliate marketing programs in the region will have to engage in a lot of training and awareness to establish flourishing affiliate networks. Also, building trust will be an important consideration before people in the region are able to collaborate as local affiliates.

Admittedly 'global' affiliate marketing platforms including Commission Junction, Amazon and ClickBank are not as established in this region as they are in the West. One of the factors that can help in the success of affiliate programs in the region is the development of new micro websites or blogs, which offer a platform for user generated material targeted to a local audience. This way, affiliates are able to funnel more traffic to a site and are thus able to see a greater return on investment for their marketing efforts.

Another approach is to combine affiliate-marketing efforts with other types of online marketing that are already prevalent in the region including cost-per-click and cost per impression. This way, marketers are able to optimize their ROI based on site visitor behavior.

In spite of the low profile of affiliate marketing, the growth of online marketing is set to create greater awareness about affiliate market. Latest trends show that new websites are being created around different topics and they are offering services that have previously been unavailable in the region's markets. This indicates that affiliate marketing is likely to take off with more and more companies and individuals creating products for distribution by merchants. Areas that are likely to attract interest from local potential affiliate partners include technology, business, fashion, travel and food.

Video Marketing

Video marketing entails the creation and distribution of online videos for the purpose of directly or indirectly promoting a brand and its product offering. Video marketing has become a popular channel through which marketers engage with their target audience due to the sheer appeal that videos may have over textual messages. Online videos also offer a cost effective channel for marketing while at the same time reaching a wider audience. Importantly it is possible to leverage the viral nature of video when users share the content across social networking platforms.

Admittedly, online video viewership is not as prominent in the MENA region when compared to global averages. Nevertheless, most web consumers use their mobile devices to view online videos, accounting for up to 72% of the online population. These users view online videos at least once each month and up to 37% access online video content through their mobile devices at least once each day.

The growth of mobile connectivity and the sheer mobile penetration in the MENA region means that that more users are able to interact frequently with digital content. With the growth of smartphones, particularly in major markets in MENA, mobile video consumption is set to rise significantly.

There are over 150 million YouTube views each day coming from MENA and one hour of video is uploaded each minute. In the UAE Google has set up a local YouTube version to cater to the growing local as well as regional video content consumption. The rapid growth in online video consumption in the region is however, limited to emerging and more liberal markets in the Gulf Arab region, in Jordan as well as in Egypt. This may be attributed to the growing Internet penetration in these countries has made it easier for users to engage with digital material. However, broadband still remains low in most of the region compared to other parts of the world such as Asia and Latin America.

In addition to the challenges of low bandwidth and Internet speeds, self-censorship in the region keeps many people, including marketers from creating digital content and online videos.

Overall, the type of video content that receives the greatest reception includes humorous and entertaining videos. While user generated content is more dominant in the region, an increasing number of major companies are beginning to leverage the potential of video for marketing. Admittedly, the region's video marketing landscape still has a long way to go but offers promising opportunities for early adopters. This is especially true for marketers who leverage the prevalent mobile video consumption to start engaging and building brand awareness with the target audience.

Other important video sites in the MENA region are: Wanda TV, ArabTube.TV and Ikbis.

A challenge that video marketers may face is the resistance to change. A large majority of one's target audience is likely to be more inclined to tangible advertisements displayed on billboards, TV and print media. However, an Econsultancy on Middle East and North Africa Digital Consumer Report indicates that up to 58% of companies in the region intend to increase their digital marketing budgets by the end of 2012.

Ecommerce

Ecommerce in the MENA region is certainly on the rise. The region is one of the growing markets for ecommerce given the progressively high Internet penetration, disposable income and high purchasing power. However, these trends vary from country to country with some countries offering more lucrative opportunities for global ecommerce than others do.

According to a recent study by the Arab Advisors Group in Jordan, the region has demonstrated laudable growth in ecommerce, in part due to improvements in broadband infrastructure. The survey also shows that an increasing number of people in the region are starting to shop online. Online shoppers in MENA are also spending more money on online purchases. In Jordan, for example, up to 25% of web users have purchased a product online or have used ecommerce services to pay for services. The total amount spent by online shoppers amounted to $370 million in 2011.

The study showed that in Egypt the number of online shoppers stands at an estimated 22.4%. Most online shoppers in Egypt purchase electronics, software, travel tickets and use ecommerce to pay subscription fees for web content. In the MENA region as a whole, online shoppers are mostly purchasing computer software and online games. This indicates that a majority of online shoppers are aged between 18 and 25 years. Euromonitor estimates that by 2014 ecommerce and online shopping will account for up to $2 billion, regionally.

For a long time, most online shoppers in the region preferred to use cash due to the prevalence of credit card fraud. However, individual countries have put in place stringent measures that have seen this type of fraud wane off. Today online shoppers largely use credit cards for their online purchases. While credit card fraud far still dominates the reasons why some users will not buy online, most users in the UAE are comfortable making online purchases. According to a survey by MasterCard Worldwide, up to eight out of ten UAE online shoppers are willing to shop online and are satisfied with their experience so far.

Buyers in the region, especially women opt to buy online due to the privacy offered by online shopping. This is particularly true for intimate purchases such as lingerie. Another factor that is pushing Internet users to make online purchase is the great deals offered by online stores.

According to data from the Nielsen Company, up to 66% of online users in the UAE are unlikely to share a negative experience they had with a brand while shopping online. Meanwhile up to 43% of consumers are greatly influenced by their networks on social media when it comes to making a purchasing decision. These consumers read product and brand reviews before deciding whether to buy a product.

Even though ecommerce shows considerable growth in the MENA region, there is room for further growth. Companies have the challenge of offering greater incentives to their target customers to encourage them to make more online purchases. 75% of the Israeli consumers that searched online will buy offline. Almost 50% of the online users in Kuwait and UAE buy online while only 20% of the Internet users in North Africa have made an online purchase.

Popular online payment methods such as PayPal are largely unavailable in the region. As such, online buyers still have to enter their credit card details on different sites; this remains one of the reasons why Internet users have not fully embraced online shopping, compared to other parts of the world. In major market such as Egypt and Saudi Arabia, pre-paid cards are a dominant method of making online payments. Dirhams, Dinars, Fils and Riyals are the prevailing currencies in this region.

According to the ecommerce provider FiftyOne, the online population in MENA represents the highest penetration of shoppers with a high purchasing power, with the average online spend being $620; this is over three times the global averages. However, a very small percentage of online shoppers engage in cross border shopping.

Popular ecommerce sites:

Given the relatively low penetration rates of ecommerce in MENA, local ecommerce sites are more popular than global or foreign ones. Some of the most popular sites are, unsurprisingly based in the region's financial center, the UAE.

www.souq.com: Is one of the largest ecommerce sites in the region and is especially popular in the UAE. Recent data shows that an upward of 25% of Souq customers is from the UAE with a large majority of the platform's users falling in 26-35 years age bracket.

www.logta.com: Was launch in 2009 and according to the Logta, the site attracts more than 11 million unique visitors each month.

www.nahel.com: Largely caters to the working class female segment in UAE. The site has progressively increased its catalogue to include over 30,000 products.

Cobone: Is the most popular daily deals platform in MENA and reportedly has a customer base of up to 1.5 million.

Conclusion

Throughout this book I have shown you that there is a real opportunity in the modern technological world in which we live to expand your once local business to a global audience. I have also however covered some of the pit-falls and mistakes that are often made when attempting to implement a global marketing strategy. Yes, the technology and therefore the target audience is now at your fingertips, however if you do not make the effort to optimize your site for that new global audience, they are unlikely to be receptive to your product offerings. If you do not consider the subtle, yet massive, impact of cultural nuances, economic differences, search engine usage and web trends along with the obvious language barriers then you are extremely unlikely to succeed in penetrating other markets.

As I have also shown you in this book there is no single global approach that can be taken when extending your business into international markets. There are many differences in the many regions of the world and I hope by covering what I see as the key global power players, that you now have a better understanding of the cultural business differences in each region.

Sometimes it's a case of trial and error however with the insights I've provided I believe you'll have more chance of succeeding.   There is definitely no magic formula when targeting a global audience however the only thing that is certain is that you must do some things differently in order to succeed. If you choose not to optimize your site and maximize your global opportunities then your site will always remain local and not global.

If you enjoyed this book, I would appreciate if you could share your feedback with other Amazon readers. If you have any questions related to the topics discussed in this book, please do not hesitate to send me an email to globalndigital@gmail.com.

As I continue my research, I will make updates to this book. As you already know, I will simply do this by adding to my book and uploading the new book to Amazon. However that means that you will not get the benefit of my new research.   Please   send   me   an   email   to globalndigital@gmail.com so I know that you are interested in receiving updated copies of this book as soon as they are released.

Gabriela Taylor

About The Author

Gabriela Taylor is an internationally educated Global Online Marketing Strategist and Consultant who's worked with some of the world's biggest brands in Telecommunications, Retail, Lifestyle and Advertising.

A recognized expert and specialist in Social Networking, Mobile Marketing and Search Engine Optimization she is fluent in 7 languages, has lived and worked in many countries throughout the world and has experience of implementing successful web-presence strategies for both startup and large established organizations.

She is the founder of Global N' Digital, a consultancy firm specializing in Online Marketing services and Cross-Cultural business practices around the world and has also published several industry related books.

*The Ultimate Guide To Marketing
Your Business With...*

*A Practical Toolkit To Unlock The Web's
Latest Social Networking Phenomenon*

GABRIELA TAYLOR

The Ultimate Guide To Building And Marketing Your Business With ...

Google

A Step By Step Guide To Unlocking The Power Of Google Tools And Maximizing Your Online Potential

GABRIELA TAYLOR

The Ultimate Guide To Building
And Marketing Your Online Business

Discover The Free Tools & Top Tips That Will Kick
Start, Grow And Maximize Your Online Business

GABRIELA TAYLOR

The Ultimate Guide To Marketing Your Business With…

*Using Tumblr To Leverage Social Buzz And Develop
A Brand Awareness Strategy For Your Business*

GABRIELA TAYLOR

Socialize To Monetize

Engaging Your Online Community Across Multiple Social Media Platforms

GABRIELA TAYLOR